FAST
BUT
LOST

Dr Pallavi Joshi, MBBS, DPM, MD, is an eminent neuropsychiatrist working in the field of mental health and has also been a corporate trainer and motivational speaker for the last 15 years. She is currently working with Manipal Hospitals, Bengaluru, and Juno Clinic. She has conducted more than 120 talks for more than 35 MNCs. She also works closely with infertility centres, conducting the programme *'Already in my heart, someday in my arms'*. Dr Pallavi's goal is to destigmatize mental health and increase awareness about various mental health disorders so that people can talk openly about them and seek treatment as well.

Dr Pallavi is a gold medallist from J.J. Group of Hospitals, Mumbai, and has received the A.K. Naik award for ground-breaking research in the psychopathology of female prisoners. She has numerous national and international publications to her name and is the author of two Marathi books—*Manachya Khol Talatun* and *Mann Aani Apan*, both dealing with mental health and the treatment of psychiatric diseases. She has a very active media presence and her opinions regarding various mental health-related issues are quoted in reputed newspapers. She also writes regularly for multiple English and Marathi newspapers.

Dr Pallavi is an artist whose paintings have been selected for various exhibitions.

Praise for the book

We may be suffering from depression and not even know about it. But there are signs from which it is possible to diagnose this condition and steps we can take to get better. Dr Pallavi Joshi's book *Fast but Lost* talks about just these signs and remedial strategies. A must-read for everyone living a busy urban life.

—**Anupam Kher,** Actor

Mental health conditions can have a substantial effect on all areas of life, such as school or work performance, relationships with family and friends and ability to participate in the community. I believe it is of utmost importance that as a society we start communicating about our mental illnesses, just like any other physical illness.

I am immensely delighted that Dr Pallavi A. Joshi acknowledged this need and put it in words in her book *Fast but Lost*. We often use the word 'depression', but do we really understand what depression is and how it affects our life, family and career and how we can get rid of it? The book talks about this in detail. I am sure it will be a beacon to many struggling with mental health.

This book will certainly start a dialogue within us. I congratulate Dr Pallavi Joshi for this initiative.

—**Amruta Fadnavis,** Singer, Social Activist and Banker

We are in a world where even the most educated shy away from words like 'mental health' and 'depression' thanks to stigmas and taboos. We sadly accept the effects of loss and trauma as 'normal' because we've been wrongly primed to confuse such acceptance of negativity with bravery and spirituality. We carry forth the negative mental effects of many other problems—marital or professional discord, divorce, failure, competition, poverty, abuse.

Dr Joshi writes about the various ways stress and adversity affect urban life, especially in the form of depression, beautifully offering her experience and wisdom about defeating this monster under the bed. An extremely useful and necessary effort for everyone, from high-flying professionals to the common man.

I wish everyone gets to read this book. For it will reset one's outlook towards life.

—**Dr Rajas Deshpande,** Director, Neurology,
Jupiter Hospital, Pune, Medical Activist and Blogger

FAST
BUT
LOST

OVERCOMING DEPRESSION IN CITY LIFE

DR PALLAVI JOSHI

Wish you Smiles ♡
— Dr. Pallavi

Published by
Rupa Publications India Pvt. Ltd 2022
7/16, Ansari Road, Daryaganj
New Delhi 110002

Sales centres:
Allahabad Bengaluru Chennai
Hyderabad Jaipur Kathmandu
Kolkata Mumbai

Copyright © Dr Pallavi Joshi 2022

The views and opinions expressed in this book are the
author's own and the facts are as reported by her which
have been verified to the extent possible, and the publishers
are not in any way liable for the same.

All rights reserved.
No part of this publication may be reproduced, transmitted,
or stored in a retrieval system, in any form or by any means,
electronic, mechanical, photocopying, recording or otherwise,
without the prior permission of the publisher.

While every effort has been made to verify the authenticity of the
information contained in this book, it is not intended as a substitute for
medical consultation with a physician. The publisher and the author are in no
way liable for the use of the information contained in this book.

ISBN: 978-93-5520-535-3

First impression 2022

10 9 8 7 6 5 4 3 2 1

The moral right of the author has been asserted.

Printed in India

This book is sold subject to the condition that it shall not,
by way of trade or otherwise, be lent, resold, hired out, or otherwise
circulated, without the publisher's prior consent, in any form of
binding or cover other than that in which it is published.

*To
Dr Nilesh Shah,
Professor and HoD, Department of Psychiatry,
Lokmanya Tilak Municipal General Hospital
and Sion Hospital, Mumbai—
Thank you for teaching me things
in and beyond psychiatry.*

CONTENTS

Foreword by Sharad Arvind Bobde / ix

1. Am I Just Sad? / 1
2. Am I at Risk? / 28
3. My Woes in the City / 48
4. Crises in My Life / 70
5. I Can Be More Resilient / 109
6. I Can Be Cured / 136
7. I Want to Live / 167
8. I Can Survive the Pandemic / 193

Acknowledgements / 214

Note: The identities of people described in the case histories have been changed to protect patient confidentiality.

FOREWORD

Emotional and mental pain is more common and less visible than physical pain. People find it hard to talk about mental pain. It is easier to say I have a fever than to say I am feeling low or anxious. Statistics show roughly 56 million Indians suffer from depression, and 38 million suffer from some anxiety disorder.

Depression kills in the long run. Covid-19 has amplified this silent pandemic, which is engulfing rural and urban areas. In India, having a mental health disorder is perceived with a sense of judgement and there is stigma associated with those having mental health issues. Realizing the implications of sound mental health, the Supreme Court, at my instance, organized mental health awareness workshops. We also had a system in place for lawyers and staff to reach out to psychologists and counsellors if they needed to.

I have known Pallavi since she was a young girl. I have watched and seen the passion to help people in her chosen field of psychiatry evolve and mature in her. All her hard work and experience has fructified into this book *Fast but Lost*. Pallavi Joshi's book is a good starting point about what depression and anxiety really are and how they originate. Through the use of case studies, she helps you to understand yourself or people around you who possibly are undergoing depression. Everyone is at risk from depression. When someone suffers from depression, friends and family members naturally want to help, but all too often their good intentions cause more harm. Awareness is the first step and this book addresses it beautifully.

—Sharad Arvind Bobde,
Former Chief Justice of India
April 2022

1

AM I JUST SAD?

'For how long have you been feeling low?'
'Umm…close to a year.'
'Are you tensed about anything?'
'Yeah…sort of! Office work, family issues, but nothing major as such.'
'Do you feel that your mood and feelings are negative most of the time? Do you find yourself feeling sad, irritated or anxious quite often?'
'Yes, almost always. I do feel happy when something good happens, but very briefly. Like it lasts for an hour or two and I start feeling sad again. I get irritated for very silly reasons. But what do you mean by anxious?'
'I mean, do you often feel restless, like something bad is going to happen to you? Also, do you get palpitations, sweating or tremors in the body during these times?'
'Yes, I do feel restless sometimes, and there is always a fear sitting at the back of my mind that things are not going well. I can feel my heart beating faster when I feel tense, but I haven't noticed sweating or tremors during these episodes.'
'Is it becoming increasingly difficult for you to focus on work?'
'Yes, lately I have been taking a lot more time to finish simple tasks in office. I also tend to forget things.'

'Do you have difficulty sleeping?'

'Yes, I cannot sleep peacefully, it's disturbed almost every day and I don't feel fresh and rejuvenated after getting up.'

'Do you get tired easily or feel fatigued more often?'

'Doctor, I'm tired *all* the time, even right after waking up.'

'Do you still enjoy doing the things which you found pleasurable?'

'I don't feel like doing anything which I used to like or enjoy doing before.'

'Do you feel there is nobody who understands what exactly you are going through?'

'I feel lonely…very lonely. In fact, I don't feel like sharing my feelings and thoughts with anyone because I feel no one really understands me.'

'Why did you take almost a year to come for help? Why did you suffer *this* long?'

'Doctor, I didn't know I have issues. In fact, me and my family thought it's just bad mood, a bad phase…just a few stressful days that will pass. In fact, my friends told me several times that I'm simply overreacting and that I should calm down. I too felt the same. However, last week when I confided in my wife that I was thinking of resigning from my job, she suggested that I meet you!'

This is a pretty common conversation that I have with my patients suffering from depression. Out of 10 such patients that I see every day, one or two definitely share this kind of story. The common strain is—we never thought it's depression, we thought it's just bad mood or just a bad phase that we are going through in life. Some of my female patients tell me, 'I thought maybe my hormones were acting crazy!'

Being a psychiatrist, what really concerns me is that many people suffer from depression for years or sometimes their entire life without recognizing that it's depression, that it's an illness that can be treated. Effective treatment can drastically improve the quality of the patient's life and that of their near ones too.

Another case that I come across, though not as frequently, is as follows.

'Doctor, she scored less marks this time in her unit test, so I guess she's going through depression.'

'Okay, is she sleeping well? Eating well?'

'Yes, all well.'

'Is she enjoying routine activities?'

'Absolutely, she enjoys watching television and even loves going out to malls.'

'Why do you think she's suffering from depression?'

'Doctor, she scored less marks in this unit test. After she saw the marksheet, she cried, and we know that feeling sad and crying can be a sign of depression.'

'Okay, let me talk to the patient alone.'

After talking to the patient, I learnt that it was just in one paper that she scored less as she didn't pace herself correctly. She cried after looking at the marksheet as she's been an overachiever, and it was just a reaction. That same evening, she went to the theatre and enjoyed watching a play with her friends. I found no signs of depression upon talking to her.

I've come across similar cases. 'My husband missed his promotion this year, too, and when I asked him about it, he got angry and shouted at me. He must be depressed!' Or, 'She broke up with her boyfriend four or five days back and she appears absent-minded. Could she be depressed or is it just momentary sadness?'

What these contrasting scenarios tell us is that many of us are not really aware of the exact nature of depression. Sometimes, people feel it's just sadness or a passing bad mood and nothing else (like in the first scenario). Sometimes, it's mistaken for momentary sadness or anger (like in the second scenario).

To combat depression and to sensitize others about it, we must first know what depression is.

So, what is depression? How does it differ from just sadness or a temporary bad mood?

A bad mood or depression?

We all feel sad and low when something bad or unwanted happens to us, but are we all depressed? Certainly not! Below are some of the key differences between sadness and depression.

- Duration of low mood

Sadness: In sadness, the low mood lasts for a pretty short duration, and is usually not associated with other features of depression like changes in sleep and appetite, low energy levels, and major changes in thinking patterns like feelings of hopelessness, helplessness and worthlessness.

Depression: In depression, low mood needs to be present for at least two weeks and is accompanied by other criteria for the same.

- Normal reaction versus abnormal state of the mind

Sadness: Sadness is marked by a normal reaction and a normal emotion to disappointing, unpleasant events that all of us experience from time to time and will keep on experiencing.

Depression: In depression, it's just not an abnormal emotion of low or negative mood; it's an abnormal mental state which influences all other areas of functioning like feeling, thinking, behaving, judgement, decision-making, etc.

- Reasons for feeling low

Sadness: We know the specific reasons behind our sadness, e.g. a failed relationship or poor performance in exams.

Depression: Reasons behind the depression may not be clear; it may happen without any external stressor.

A triggering or stressful event may or may not be present in depression. In endogenous depression, there are no external stressors; meaning, in this kind of depression, we are unable to find any external cause for it. This is the case with almost 25 per cent of the total cases of depression.[1]

I remember the example of the famous Bollywood actress Deepika Padukone, who is now an advocate for depression awareness. In an interview, she stated,

> …I had won all my awards and you know all the appreciation for 2013, everything had happened and it was a great time and obviously at once one gonna think like why is she depressed, she has everything going for her. But, I woke up one morning just feeling empty you know like this pittish feeling in my stomach that I was telling them that I get this pittish feeling in my stomach. I woke up like feeling directionless, I didn't know where to go, I didn't know what to do and I had these bouts of feeling so low that I would just start crying at the drop of a hat…[2]

---

[1] 'Endogenous Depression', *Comprehensive Clinical Psychology*, ScienceDirect, 1998, https://bit.ly/3tYuUNb. Accessed on 16 March 2022.

[2] '"I Felt Empty and Directionless", Says Deepika Padukone on Her Battle with Depression: Full Transcript', NDTV, 22 March 2015, https://bit.ly/3MXdRDO. Accessed on 16 March 2022.

In endogenous depression, one may have intrinsic hormonal disturbances such as disturbances of the thyroid. In exogenous depression, yes, external stressors are present, but often these are just a starting event and the illness persists even when the stressor is gone. Even simple, routine activities become stressful with time in such cases.

- Interest in the activities which you like to do

Sadness: In sadness, interest in pleasurable activities remains intact, such as shopping, watching movies or hanging out with friends.

Depression: Depression is marked by a loss of interest in all previously enjoyable activities. I remember the example given by a patient who got cured of depression. He told me, 'Doctor, going to office on Monday was always a pain and I never considered my reduced interest in day-to-day activities and lower focus at work as a sign of depression. I thought I was fine, but sometime later, when a plan for a trip to Goa did not excite me, I knew something was seriously wrong with me and I came to you for evaluation.'

- Changes in sleep and appetite

Sadness: The low mood doesn't affect activities like sleeping or eating routines. In fact, sadness or stress may lead a person to overeat or indulge in eating more sweets and chocolates, as stress increases the craving for something sweet and chocolates have stress-busting neurotransmitters such as anandamide and tryptophan.

Depression: Generally, a depressed person will have a disturbed sleep. There can be difficulty in falling asleep or maintaining sleep, and they may not feel fresh after waking up in the morning.

There is less interest in eating too. If the depression advances, the patient may eat very little and experience profound disinterest in eating. In some cases, the patient may tend to sleep a lot and eat large amounts of food. This may happen in a variant of depression called 'atypical depression'.

- Socio-occupational deterioration

Sadness: This is a very important criterion. We may have thoughts like: 'Oh, I don't feel happy nowadays', 'Life is pretty stressed' or 'Of late, people find me boring'. But as long as we are able to function well in our social and occupational circle, that is, are able to work properly and maintain our relationships well, it does not indicate a serious issue.

Depression: There is deterioration in work performance. Social and family relations too may suffer.

- Thoughts of guilt and regret

Sadness: There is an appropriate sense of guilt or regret owing to a mistake, but it is limited to that event only.

Depression: There is an overall feeling of failure, multiple regrets and inappropriate guilt about things the patient is not even actually responsible for.

- Depressogenic thinking

Sadness: In sadness, there are no thoughts like hopelessness about the future, helplessness about the situation and worthlessness about overall life. There is clarity of thought.

Depression: All patients have at least one of the three important depressogenic thoughts mentioned above and, in addition, have other distorted thoughts like overgeneralization, which means feeling that if one bad situation happens once, it will happen again and again; maximization, where external problems are glorified and minimization, i.e. the feeling that your strengths are minimal and your achievements are insignificant.

- Associated features of anxiety

Sadness: There will be no symptoms of anxiety, like a constant feeling of restlessness or the fear that something bad is going to happen.

Depression: It invariably comes with anxiety until it reaches a terminal state, where there is no anxiety. The majority of patients report restlessness, fears of known or unknown things and the sense that something bad is going to happen. There may be free-floating anxiety which the patient feels throughout the day or on-and-off episodic anxiety issues, which are associated with rapid heartbeat, cold and sweaty hands and feet, and dryness of the mouth.

- Suicidal thoughts, suicide attempts, self-harm

Sadness: There are no extreme thoughts like self-harm or suicidal ideas, as sadness is a normal emotion and doesn't involve serious disturbance with thoughts and doesn't reach the extreme of any emotion including sadness.

Depression: In depression, depending on the severity, the patient may have desires to harm themselves, express suicidal ideas or there may be attempts to harm or kill themselves.

- Multiple undiagnosed body pains

Sadness: Sadness is not associated with body pains or other complaints related to the body.

Depression: There could be multiple body pains, for which the cause may not be known/detected through blood or imaging tests. Yet, they will persist and are very much real. They can be addressed as well, but only if we address depression first. Why do they happen in depression? When we are happy, we still have minor pains or discomforts in the body, but we don't normally pay attention to them or recognize them. When suffering from depression, the pain, which may be a three on a scale of 10, becomes a 10/10. Stress increases the pain perception as well. Also, the mechanism called nociception becomes active when we are depressed. This is when the pathway in the body which conveys unpleasant sensations becomes hyperactive, so that more and more unpleasant sensations are conveyed. Some antidepressants have an excellent action on pain pathways and uplift the mood as well. So they can be used to treat this condition.

Signs to watch out for

What are the criteria that we use to diagnose depression? These are given by the *Diagnostic and Statistical Manual* for diagnosing psychiatry illnesses by the American Psychiatric Association. In psychiatry, we usually do not use blood or imaging tests. Our diagnosis relies heavily on what our patients and their relatives tell us and what we observe in the patient. These standardized criteria are helpful in distinguishing depression from other similar conditions such as sadness, bad moods, mood swings or temper issues.

These standardized criteria, also given by the International Classification of Diseases (ICD) and the *Diagnostic and Statistical Manual of Mental Disorders* (DSM), help avoid situations where one psychiatrist diagnoses a condition as depression and another feels that it's something else. These criteria provide uniformity in diagnosis and allow the severity to be assessed. For a diagnosis of depression, five or more of these criteria need to be fulfilled. Some extra features not mentioned in the criteria also aid in diagnosis, which experts use from time to time.

These standardized criteria/symptoms are mentioned below. Any five of these symptoms must be visible in the patient for longer than two weeks for a diagnosis.

i. Depressed or low mood: The low mood must be persistent for most of the time on most days. Even a depressed patient may feel good for a while when something positive happens, but they quickly revert to the low mood. The mood is negative for most patients, ranging from sad, low and irritable to anxious.
ii. Markedly diminished interest or pleasure in most or all activities: A patient will notice that they are unable to enjoy routine activities. What is more bothersome is that they are unable to derive pleasure from the activities they previously enjoyed. These are of course different for everyone, but usually patients lose interest in their hobbies, in going out with friends or watching movies.
iii. Significant weight loss (or poor appetite) or weight gain: A change of more than 5 per cent of body weight in a month, when not dieting or putting any special efforts for weight loss or gain will be seen in the patient. (We generally see weight loss in depressed patients.)
iv. Insomnia or hypersomnia: Usually in depression, there is difficulty in maintaining sleep, and the patient may get up two or three hours earlier in the morning than their usual time. When depression is accompanied by anxiety, a person might find it difficult to fall asleep.

Many patients report unrestful sleep as well, where there is no feeling of freshness after waking up. Excessive sleep is usually seen in atypical depression (discussed below).

v. Psychomotor retardation or agitation: A patient may observe that they have slowed down or appear restless. In case of retardation, they may notice they are taking longer to finish certain tasks and in the case of agitation, they may find it difficult to focus due to negative thoughts and the constant urge to move around, among others. Relatives may also mention that the patient takes more time to finish certain activities or takes time to answer simple questions (in cases of psychomotor retardation). In cases of agitation, relatives may report that the patient is observed fidgeting in the chair or pacing around the home most of the time.

vi. Fatigue or loss of energy: Most patients report that they get tired easily or don't feel energetic. A neurochemical imbalance, low levels of the neurohormones responsible for cheerfulness and constant overthinking make them prone to easy fatiguability.

vii. Feelings of worthlessness or excessive or inappropriate guilt: Depression leads to a magnification of problems and a minimization of strengths. This may lead a patient to feel like a failure or worthless or guilty unnecessarily.

viii. Diminished ability to think or concentrate, or indecisiveness: Patients invariably report difficulty in focusing at work and taking time to take simple decisions and resolve mental dilemmas. This typically happens as the emotional mind hijacks the intellectual mind and the executive functions of the brain like decision-making, judgement and concentration slow down.

ix. Recurrent thoughts of death (not just fear of dying), or suicidal ideation, planning or attempt: This one is a severe symptom and often warrants immediate medical attention. Any expressed thoughts of ending one's life or any suicide attempt should not be ignored and the patient must be taken to a psychiatrist as soon as possible.

Suicide is the second leading cause of death among young people aged 15–29 years and all attempts should be made to read the cues of impending suicide.[3] According to the Centers for Disease Control and Prevention (CDC) WISQARS Leading Causes of Death Reports (2019), suicide was the second leading cause of death among individuals between the ages of 10 and 34 in the US, and the fourth leading cause of death among individuals between the ages of 35 and 44.[4] An entire chapter has been dedicated later in the book to understanding suicide and its prevention.

Other symptoms a patient may have are reduced sexual drive, restlessness and other anxiety features like something bad may happen. When depression is severe, there may be some signs of madness—a patient may hear voices not audible to others, telling them that they are responsible for bad things happening or that they should end their life.

Depending on the severity of the symptoms, depression is often categorized as mild, moderate and severe. The treatments differ as per the severity.

One illness, many faces

Depression has some variants. Although they look different at the surface, it is typical depression which leads to these symptoms.

---

[3]'Suicide: one person dies every 40 seconds', World Health Organization (WHO), 9 September 2019, https://bit.ly/362Y2ej. Accessed on 16 March 2022.
[4]National Institute of Mental Health (NIMH), Suicide Statistics, https://bit.ly/3LVemNw. Accessed on 12 April 2022.

Different, but still the same depression

Sneha, a 20-year-old woman, made a visit to the psychiatry clinic by herself. She was sleeping almost 8–10 hours a day, had gained more than 5 kilograms in the last three months, was having a constant craving for carbohydrates (carbs), binge eating desserts and fried foods and had difficulty in controlling these urges. In fact, she said she used to feel good temporarily after binging on these high-calorie foods, but felt guilty later. She would feel a certain heaviness in the body for hours. She would react to simple issues with irritation and crying. Her family members told her that she had no self-control and discipline and that she was gaining weight because of that. Because of the weight gain she was sleeping a lot more and often felt lethargic, leaving her all the more irritated.

When I spoke to her, I found out that she was experiencing a persistent low mood and high irritability. She was losing interest in everything that she used to like before and would feel tired most of the time. Food was not just a matter of interest; it was a compulsion, and the same was true for uncontrollable sleep too. 'She is sleeping and eating well, how can she be depressed?' her family members wondered. This, in turn, made her feel like no one understood her. She felt even more hurt upon listening to the concerns and remarks of her dear ones. She blamed herself for not being able to fight the blues, losing hope about having a good life.

This is one face of depression with somewhat unusual features. Hence, it is called atypical depression. Most of the time, this kind of depression is characterized by a reversal of vegetative symptoms, meaning that instead of the sleeplessness and appetite loss in typical depression, the patient experiences excessive sleep and increased appetite along with weight gain.

The patient's mood is still 'reactive', meaning that they still react appropriately to emotionally stimulating experiences and hence there can be delay in referral by other doctors. But if we ask the patient about the symptoms in detail, all features of depression are eventually revealed.

Pain behind a smile

A dear friend and colleague of Vikas Bhat, a 45-year-old man working at a very high post in a multinational company (MNC), observed 'changes' in him in the last six months. He was brought by that friend to the psychiatry outpatient department (OPD). The friend observed that although Bhat completed his work efficiently, attended office parties and interacted with everyone formally, somewhere he appeared lost. They hadn't been playing tennis on weekends of late, which they used to enjoy before. During our conversation, the patient agreed that he had to push himself for everything, as every task felt like a burden. Although he was meeting all the deadlines, he was taking more time than usual. He wasn't showing it, but he was losing interest in previously pleasurable activities. He had started questioning the purpose of the majority of life events. He did not come to meet a mental health care provider on his own as he felt he would be able to overcome it on his own.

This is called 'smiling depression'. Although the patient suffers from depression, outwardly he appears happy and satisfied. He has minimal problems at his job or in his relationships, but that doesn't mean he is not suffering. Such patients hide their suffering very well when they are in public and make it seem as if everything is fine with their life, but in fact the depression is taking a big toll on their life. Also, they have to put more effort than usual to keep concentration at work, to meet deadlines and to maintain social and family relationships. Most of the time, a close relative or friend can still understand the difference in the person in terms of what they were before and how they are now and brings the patient to us.

Not drama, but a call for help

Suneeta, a middle-aged woman, was referred to the psychiatry OPD after undergoing extensive investigations in the neurology OPD for features suggestive of fits or seizures. Nothing was found on the investigations. When we asked the patient a few questions, we came to know that such episodes have always happened in front of people but never when the patient was alone or asleep. The patient never injured herself during such episodes, which were precipitated by some tensions in the family. The patient appeared depressed, and this is usually a response to intolerable stress.

We often see patients who get bouts of seizures, who say that they are suddenly unable to see from one eye, have excruciating pain near the abdomen, etc. The relatives feel that they are being dramatic. But that's far from the truth. It's not drama at all, nor are they being dramatic. In fact, for any underlying hysterical episode, there is always a psychiatric condition, and most of the time, it's depression. Due to depression and lack of attention from the family, many patients get this 'unconscious split' when stressed. This happens unknowingly—they don't do it consciously. In fact, it's a cry for help. When we address their concerns and depression, they are able to handle the stress in a better manner.

I forget a lot

Prasenjit, a 30-year-old man, visited our OPD. He was working in a software company as a project manager. For a couple of months, he had been having difficulty remembering certain things discussed in meetings. He would forget simple stuff like where he had put his glasses or keys or his mobile and was wasting a lot of time finding them. Lately, he had even forgotten what he was saying in meetings and had to take some time to orient himself again. This had happened not once, but twice. His project's deadline was approaching, and he had not been able to sleep well for the last few weeks and even had difficulty focusing. He was feeling low in confidence and had low energy levels. He was really worried about the future, as his performance kept deteriorating. On further enquiry, we found that he was fulfilling all the criteria of depression, although the concerning symptom for him was only forgetfulness.

The patient's complaint is often forgetfulness for routine things, and they may feel that they are experiencing true memory loss or dementia. In depression, there is no actual memory loss; what we have is absent-mindedness. The patient is so self-absorbed that they don't even register many things. That's why there is no recall. But the patient will give you details of their memory loss—they are concerned as they know they are not doing well in the socio-occupational sphere and feel a great deal of distress. A dementia patient will never be concerned about their memory loss. In fact, they might not even be aware of it.

Other symptoms of depression can be found upon enquiry, such as low moods, feeling like a failure, hopelessness and helplessness. There will never be major incidents of forgetfulness, like forgetting one's home address or forgetting the identity of important people in their life, which happens in dementia.

If you ask a depressed patient with forgetfulness what they had for breakfast the previous day, they might not be able to recall, and the fact that they are unable to recall will leave them feeling disturbed. But if you ask a dementia patient the same thing, they too may say that they don't remember, but they will not be concerned with the fact that their memory is failing. They might even fabricate the facts (this never happens in depression), what's called confabulation in medicine, by giving false information that they don't recollect. They might say, 'I had poha' when they had just tea, or sometimes they may even try to fill colours in those falsifications by saying, 'Oh, it was a wonderful morning, we had an elaborate breakfast', and so on. Also, the onset of forgetfulness in dementia is very slow and deteriorates gradually, unlike depression, where it starts abruptly.

Depression or anxiety disorder?

Ananya, a 24-year-old woman, came to our OPD. She had a history of recurrent anxiety attacks and symptoms of restlessness, palpitations and shaking of the body during attacks. She had been suffering from these attacks multiple times a day, lasting for about 5 minutes, for the last 20 days. She had come from a small town to this city for work three months back. She was living as a paying guest and was finding it difficult to cope with the stress of the daily commute, and 10–12 hours of work, plus training. She was feeling suffocated. She had difficulty falling asleep and would wake up in the middle of night because of recurrent nightmares about missing the office bus or being late to work. For the last month, she had been feeling low and anxious throughout the day. She said her colleagues were good, but she could not establish friendships with any of them because there was simply no time. She hadn't been feeling like calling old friends lately, even on weekends. She was worried about the future, as joining this company had been her dream. She was feeling disillusioned with the current situation and did not know how she would spend the rest of the days in this city. She reported that she felt very lonely and had crying spells almost every day.

These symptoms might suggest anxiety, but there was an underlying depression in her case. When we prescribed medicines to her along with some behavioural remedies, she asked us as to why we were prescribing antidepressants when her symptoms were those of anxiety.

Unlike the popular belief that anxiety and depression are two distinct disorders, they have a major overlap. Almost all patients of depression have some degree of anxiety except those with terminal-stage depression, where there is no anxiety, as the person is beyond that. The anxiety in the early–moderate stages of depression occurs through similar pathways in the brain as depression. Hence, the medicines given are also the same in most of the cases. Also, many cases of severe anxiety have an additional diagnosis of depression, as severe anxiety leads to poor functioning in different spheres and helplessness, which, in turn, cause depression.

Mood changes with the weather

In polar countries, where there is no sunlight for months at a stretch, the people often suffer from depression. This is called seasonal affective disorder, and it usually recurs every year during the same time. Its symptoms are mood changes with the onset of the winter season, with associated features like excessive sleeping and poor energy levels. Usually, phototherapy or light therapy is the treatment of choice in these cases, as the depression responds to light treatment very quickly.

'I occupy one pole of this swinging disorder'

We hear this phrase so often! 'I think I have bipolar disorder' or 'He has so many mood swings that it looks like he is bipolar'. But most of the time, what people are talking about are mood swings and not the actual bipolar disorder. As opposed to popular notion, typical bipolar disorder doesn't have mood swings like depression in the morning and mania in the evening.

Dhriti, a 20-year-old college student, had a history of overfamiliarity (i.e. showing excessive familiarity with lesser-known or unknown people), reduced sleep, excessive spending and bragging. Her mood would swing from happy to irritated without any stressor prior to this behaviour. She was brought to us by her parents as this was happening for 10 days. We began talking, and she was unstoppable once she began—she said she knows our prime minister and has important contacts, that she has some special powers and people are jealous of her because of her beauty and intelligence. She had started smoking a week back. We found out that she had a history of depression a year back and had responded to antidepressants, which she was still taking. She also had a family history of depression in her mother.

Bipolar type 1 is characterized by mania, which has symptoms like an expansive mood, excessive happiness, boasting about oneself, decreased need for sleep, very high energy levels, overfamiliarity, excessive talkativeness with strangers, novelty-seeking behaviours like trying new drugs, substances or promiscuity and excessive spending. The other pole is depression, which has all the features of classic depression. In between the two poles, the patient is totally asymptomatic and normal. Many people think the episodes of mania alternate with depression, but it usually does not happen like this. An episode of mania can follow mania, and depression can follow depression. The episodes can last for months without treatment, but patients may show improvement in a matter of weeks with proper treatment. In bipolar 1, the patient's relatives often tend to overlook the episodes of depression which happen after a few episodes of mania, as mania consumes much energy and requires a lot more vigilance from them. They often feel that if the patient is silent and a little aloof, they are not in much distress.

Bipolar type 2 is characterized by several episodes of depression for years and if the relatives of the patient are vigilant, then occasionally, maybe once or twice in a lifetime, they may notice a hypomanic episode, which is a very milder version of mania. In this, energy levels are high, the patient may be very talkative, spending excessively and be in a happy mood. But there is no socio-occupational deterioration, meaning they are still able to function normally at their workplace, and their social functioning remains intact as well.

The mind causes physical pain

Sudha, a 45-year-old woman from the lower-middle socio-economic stratum, came to see us after many physicians and surgeons asked her to meet a psychiatrist for her symptoms. For the last two years, she had been having on-and-off back pain, abdominal pain and bloating, headache and tightness in the shoulders and neck. She also had tingling and numbness in both hands and feet and sometimes felt a burning sensation while passing urine. She felt weak overall. She reported that she had been feeling weak and sick for a long time. She said she was raised by a dominating father and her husband, who works in a contractual job, was also very demanding and dominating. She had been working tirelessly since her childhood. Although the physical work wasn't really expected from her now, she felt drained by simple household tasks too. Her two kids were attending college in another city.

We see many people with undiagnosed pains in the body or with troublesome symptoms which are not explained by medical science. They visit multiple doctors for the pain and undergo several tests, but nothing comes of it. Finally, they take a call to visit a psychiatrist. On enquiry, we find all features of depression, but those are never the patient's primary complaints. One should also note that in the Indian scenario, it's easier to talk about and get treated for a headache or body aches than depression.

The mechanism of different pains in depression has been described earlier, and both depression and pain respond very well to antidepressants.

Those temper tantrums are a sign

Muralidhar, a 75-year-old patient, was brought to us by his relatives. For the last two months, he had been having bouts of anger every two to three days, and even more frequently against the caretaker. In these two months, two caretakers had left the job because of his extreme irritability and temper issues. He was not sleeping properly and would often ask the caretaker to massage his legs and back every hour. He was also drinking more frequently in the evenings. When his relatives refused him drinks, he would get more irritated. Although he was eating properly, he had difficulty in passing motion. The day before the consultation he had even thrown his food out of the window in a fit of anger as he had found it tasteless. He was found sobbing twice or thrice in his room, refusing to admit the reason. He reported no issues with memory. On talking to the patient, we found him to be a little uncooperative initially. Then we spoke a little about tennis, which he used to watch regularly till a few months back. Then gradually, he opened up about his feelings. We found that the new caretakers were unable to understand his needs. He was unable to talk to them properly due to language issues, leaving him frustrated and lonely. He wished to sleep for at least eight hours a night, but was finding it difficult to get good sleep for even five hours. Alcohol helped him sleep, and that's why he asked for it every day. He said he had multiple body pains lately and constipation was really bothering him. The feeling of frustration and helplessness triggered anger. He shared that he was feeling hopeless, helpless and worthless and was having markedly reduced energy and reduced interest in all activities.

These are the symptoms of agitated depression. Often, people suffering from this type of depression come to us for anger management, but behind these anger spells there usually are negative emotions, dissatisfaction and frustration with life. Many patients who go through depression may go into a shell, but some express their depression through aggression. In fact, we make sure to evaluate all patients referred to us for anger management for depression as well, as often it's the major cause of the agitation.

Affecting different populations

Children

The symptoms of depression in children are often not classic. They may present unusual symptoms depending on their age. Younger children may present regressed behaviour, for example, a five-year-old child may start behaving like a two-year-old and starts urinating and defecating in their clothes. Older children may refuse to go to school and have a variety of pain symptoms with no apparent cause, frequent nightmares, poor scholastic performance and high irritability. In severe cases, even growth may be retarded. However, it's easy to diagnose depression in such cases through a clinical interview. A plethora of symptoms of depression can also emerge in such cases.

Teens

When suffering from depression, teens may show social aloofness, addictions, recklessness, poor scholastic performance, sleep and appetite disturbances, anger outbursts, low confidence and self-esteem issues.

Most teenagers go through an identity crisis, where they struggle to establish their identity. It's a phase of distantiation from parents, and they rebel against authority figures to some extent. These are usually not indicative of depression. But this is also the age when most psychiatric disorders manifest for the first time, and their symptoms could be different, so when in doubt, it's a good idea to get it evaluated by a psychiatrist.

The elderly

Depression usually presents itself with poor self-care, self-neglect, multiple body pains and a lack of interest in routine. It may be accompanied by severe anxiety issues like restlessness, fearfulness and sometimes psychotic features like extreme unshakable false beliefs, say, the world is coming to an end or that all their money has been stolen.

Post-partum women

Priyanka, a 32-year-old female patient, was referred by her gynaecologist for lack of sleep, refusal to breastfeed the baby, and for angry and aggressive behaviour with her family members. The patient would either cry or get angry most of the time, often shouting that this child was not wanted and that she could never become a good mother and wanted to die. She delivered the baby a month back. It was her first child, a boy. Initially, the family thought that it was baby blues, and that with time, everything would get better. On the contrary, things gradually worsened, and the patient was brought to us for evaluation and treatment.

Almost 15–85 per cent women face low moods post childbirth.[5] This happens due to a sudden shift of hormones after childbirth as well as the shift in circumstances and the additional responsibility that the new life brings. Barring easy tearfulness, little lows and absent-mindedness, most of the time no other symptoms are seen, and baby blues disappear on their own after two weeks. Only support and psychoeducation are needed, and these are often given by older women in the family. But post-partum depression is an entirely different entity and needs to be addressed immediately for the sake of the safety and well-being of the baby and the mother. Almost 10 per cent of women experience it, and this should be suspected when the baby blues continue even after a couple of weeks after delivery.[6] Apparent symptoms are severe mood swings, irritability, lack of bonding with the baby, feelings of inappropriate guilt, self-harming and baby-harming thoughts. It's often associated with a history of mood disorders (depression and/or mania) in the family or even in the patient. This condition needs to be treated very skillfully by consulting a psychiatrist.

Women facing menstrual cycle changes

A low degree of depression, anxiety and mood swings happens to almost 75–80 per cent of women in the premenstrual phase, typically starting three–seven days before their period.[7] This

---

[5] Pearlstein, Teri et al., 'Postpartum depression', *Am J Obstet Gynecol.*, April 2009; 200(4): 357–64, https://bit.ly/3M0HS4j. Accessed on 12 April 2022.
[6] Sadock, Benjamin James and Virginia Alcott Sadock, *Synopsis of Psychiatry*, 10th edition, Indian reprint, Lippincott Williams & Wilkins, 2007.
[7] Ibid.

is associated with feelings of heaviness in the body due to water retention, pain in the breasts, breakouts on the skin and craving for sweet and oily food. Psychological symptoms such as excessive irritability, low moods, reduced sleep and crying spells may also appear. These symptoms happen due to a fall in the levels of the oestrogen hormone in the body. One area in the brain—the limbic system, which is responsible for the emotional component of an individual, is very sensitive to oestrogen levels in the body. Hence, symptoms relating to the mind are produced. Bodily symptoms are linked with the fall in oestrogen and increase in progesterone. We usually don't treat these premenstrual syndrome (PMS) symptoms with medicines until and unless it has a severe effect with criteria meeting the diagnosis of depression in the premenstrual period. In such cases, antidepressants are very useful. For general symptoms of PMS, reducing salt intake and increasing physical activity during this period often reduces the symptoms. Sometimes, a supplement such as primrose oil can also be given, which helps reduce physical and mental symptoms.

Myths and facts

Myth: Depression happens to mentally weak people.

Fact: Nobody is immune to depression. In fact, I would say that people who try to remain too strong for too long, much beyond their threshold, may eventually suffer from depression.

Myth: Depression is not real, as the mind is not an organ and can't get diseased.

Fact: Although intangible, depression is as real as any other illness of the body. The mind is very much a complex system and is an expression of the brain function. Every neuropsychiatric disease has a biological basis, and so does depression. With developments in neuroradiology, we know the exact areas and the exact circuits in the brain that are affected by depression and also the exact neurotransmitters that regulate them. So, although some domains of the mind still remain a mystery, the disturbance caused by depression is quite clear.

Myth: Depressed people are lazy.

Fact: Depressed people are not lazy, but in one kind of depression, lethargy and amotivation are the symptoms—this is called 'retarded depression'. This kind of depression makes patients behave like that. In such cases, laziness has nothing to do with the person's temperament. In another kind of depression where anxiety is predominant, a person may be thinking so much that it manifests in physical tiredness. In fact, an anxious-depressed person thinks way more than a healthy individual.

Myth: Depression or any mental illness is a fruit of bad past deeds.

Fact: In Indian culture, people believe in karma and often say that bad things happen to people who do evil and good things happen to people who do good. Even a person who goes through depression often believes that to be a fact and accepts it as a part of karma. In fact, depression can happen to anyone and has definite biological basis, just like any other disorder.

Myth: Children don't get depressed. They are too young to go through depression.

Fact: No age is immune to depression. At and above five years, a child is able to express depression. They may feel it even earlier but may not be able to express it like adults. There are ways to identify it nonetheless. Although underreported, childhood depression is quite common and even more common in the stresses of urban life.

Myth: Men never get depressed; this illness affects only women.

Fact: Although the prevalence of depression is less in men than in women, men do get depressed.[8] Due to societal pressure, they are more reluctant to seek help, as they are expected to remain strong in all circumstances. Sometimes they don't even recognize, label and verbalize their feelings and emotions properly, so the depression among them is often underreported. They often have more severe symptoms that are detected many months or years after the onset of depression.

Myth: Depression is a result of a bad and non-nutritious diet.

Fact: Although diet has some role to play in depression treatment, particularly as an add-on measure, depression happens in all socio-economic strata, where nutrition status varies. Depression has a much more complex causation than mere diet.

Myth: As my mother or father had depression, I am surely going to develop it.

Fact: Although genetic link plays a significant role in the development of depression, it is caused by several other factors, such as adverse experiences, resilience of the person to deal with it, hormonal influences and other medical disorders. Family history is just a risk factor.

---

[8] Ibid.

2
AM I AT RISK?

The typical questions we hear are, 'Doctor, why me?' or 'Do you really think I can go through depression? I have been so strong all my life.' Then, at the end of the session, the patient's spouse or some other relative typically asks, 'Doctor, you explained the plan and symptoms well, but why does this depression happen?'

We also hear questions like, 'Doctor, I am going through more than her in my life currently, she just has to manage the home. I am earning well, and our children are independent now. In fact, if someone has to be stressed among the two of us, it should be me, who is paying all the loans, doing the office work. This woman has been through a lot in our earlier days of married life. And now when things are going well, how can she go through depression? I don't understand.'

Coming to the question why depression happens, there isn't just one answer. It varies from person to person. There are risk factors and vulnerable people, but it's not dependent on one causative factor. There are no simple answers when we ask about the pathology of depression, unlike when we are talking about swine flu, which is caused by the virus H1N1. As regards the cause of depression, there isn't a single and definite answer.

I remember one of my senior psychiatrist friends used to ask this question in a jocular way, 'If a mosquito bites you and you get malaria, do you go and ask the mosquito "why did you bite me"?' No, nobody does that. All we can do is use preventive strategies when it comes to mosquito-borne diseases, particularly when we live or travel in high-risk areas. Similarly, we can all use preventive strategies to build our resilience and reduce stress. If we fall in a high-risk category for depression, such as experiencing major stress in life after having faced some trauma, which is causing difficulty in our day-to-day functioning, we should do timely damage control by contacting a mental healthcare provider. Just as infections can happen to anyone and everyone, no one is immune to depression.

But yes, certain factors make you more prone to depression. However, these are just risk factors, and it is not necessary that you too will end up with depression. For example, consuming alcohol every day increases the risk of having liver ailments and cirrhosis, but not every alcoholic faces these issues. So, while the risk factors of depression (like past traumas, family history and childhood adversities, among others) definitely increase your odds of getting an associated illness and should be avoided wherever possible (though genetics and adversities are largely beyond one's control), not having them doesn't make you immune to depression, nor does it guarantee the onset of depression.

We know exactly what goes wrong in the neurochemistry of the brain and in neuronal communications, and issues at the level of neurotransmitters and their interplay are the final common pathway in every case of depression. Still, when we ask what has gone wrong, in each and every case the answer is a conglomeration of multiple factors—biological-psychological-social-spiritual.

And depression is not the only illness in medical science where exact causative factors are not known—there are several others too. In fact, for the majority of non-communicable diseases, the exact aetiology is not known, as with cancers, heart diseases, thyroid disorders, brain strokes, etc. We can prevent these illnesses to a great extent by controlling the risk factors, but it's not foolproof. In many of these diseases, we know who is at risk due to the presence of multiple associated risk factors and we can advise the patients to quit or control their risky behaviour and modify their lifestyle to reduce the risk of contracting these diseases. The same applies to depression too.

One more point to note is that there are some risk factors which can be controlled—what we call 'modifiable risk factors', for example, when we shed extra weight, it reduces the risk of heart diseases. However, there are some unmodifiable risk factors, such as a family history of depression or heart disease, wherein we need to accept the associated risk, as these factors cannot be modified. Yet, these remain just risk factors, as issues at the genetic level do not always express themselves.

Now coming back to the questions: 'My relative has much fewer stressors than me, then how come they had this breakdown?' or 'My colleague seems better placed than me, then how come this is happening to them?' The simple answer to this is that we cannot gauge the stress a person is under by any standard measure. In fact, perception of stress is a highly individual experience and is often not predictable. So, someone may have a breakdown with what you call a minimum tension and may have greater tolerance to a stress which is unbearable for you. For example, I have seen people breaking down at some insult in the office and handling their own or a dear relative's serious illness bravely.

Coming back to the question: when I have handled so much in my life, so much tension and stressors, how did this simple stress lead to a breakdown? Let us take an example. Suppose a table has a capacity to bear a load of 200 kilograms and is carrying 190 kilograms. Then, an additional load of 30 kilograms was added, leading to a breakdown. We cannot then hold this minor weight of 30 kilograms responsible for the breakdown. In the process of saturation of stress, minor wear and tear had begun with the previous weight, but this new minor stress was the final blow, the final nail in the coffin, so to speak.

Also, if one leg of this table is broken, it may collapse with even less stress and much earlier than expected. If the table is aged and has borne a lot of traumas, it will be even more prone to early breakdown. Similarly, if a person has some genetic or familial factors responsible for depression and has gone through a lot of psychosocial traumas, even small adversities will further reduce their stress tolerance, making them prone to depression at much lower stress levels.

Genetics

How does genetics play a role in depression?

According to various clinical studies, if one parent is suffering from depression, then a child has a risk of 10–25 per cent of developing depression as well. If both parents have a history of depression or any other mood disorder, then the risk of depression goes up to 50 per cent in the child.[9] The more severe the illness in the previous generation, the more significant is the risk to children in the same family. A strong association was found on some of the changes in loci on the specific chromosomes of depressed patients and their clinical depression, showing a very strong linkage of genetic link to depression.

---

[9]Sadock, Benjamin James and Virginia Alcott Sadock, *Synopsis of Psychiatry*, 10th edition, Indian reprint, Lippincott Williams & Wilkins, 2007.

Seeds sown in childhood

Most of the studies and our clinical observations state that the loss of a parent before the age of 11 is a predictor of depression in adulthood. The loss of a parent takes a big toll on a child's developing mind, and the circumstances, which invariably follow that event, also affect their childhood.

Child abuse: Verbal, physical and sexual

Verbal and physical abuse definitely lower a child's self-esteem, particularly if it happens repeatedly and without an attempt to show love and appreciation for the child's good qualities. If you beat children or repeatedly put them down, they might not hate you, but they start hating themselves. Low self-esteem and a negative self-image are big predictors of depression in adult life.

The problem with sexual abuse is even more complex and has several facets. And the irony is that it is the victim who suffers from guilt and shame, not the perpetrators.

In most cases, physical abuse is reported as being perpetrated by the mother, while most intra-family sexual abuse is often reported to be perpetrated by uncles or the father.[10]

Physical abuse has not been considered a matter of concern in traditional Indian households for many generations. Beating children has been considered normal, and parents even think that it should be done to keep a child on the right track. It has been believed that a certain amount of strictness and punishment is necessary to curtail non-desirable behaviour. However, repeated or harsh physical abuse has a negative impact on the child's psyche, and they may become less confident, indecisive, depressed, scared to express themselves or lonely. They may also start hating their parents later and become

---

[10]Ibid.

immune to punishments. They might turn rebellious, or may form a similar group of friends. Ultimately, they may become less sensitive to violence. Hence, this should be avoided.

The impact of child sexual abuse depends on various factors such as who did it, at what age it started and for how long it continued and also the psyche of the abused child. The closer the biological relationship of the abuser with the victim, the longer the duration of the abuse and the earlier it started in the child's life, the greater the trauma the child bears. They may face the inability to get intimate with their partners in the future, and may suffer from post-traumatic stress disorder (PTSD), depression, phobias and in extreme cases, suicidality. They often have mistrust and confusion about relationships.

Parental neglect

The fourth form of abuse is parental neglect, often perceived by children who were raised in urban settings, where both parents in a nuclear family work. The perceived absence of parents, that is, if the child feels that either parent is physically or emotionally absent in their growing years, may lead to the child feeling neglected and developing anxiety at that time or even later. In child development, the mother signifies love to the child and the father signifies trust and security. If the mother is psychologically absent, the child has a higher risk of developing depression, and if the father is psychologically absent, then the child is more likely to develop anxiety and trust issues.

Social issues in childhood

If the child was bullied to an intolerable extent for any reasons such as wearing spectacles, being obese or being an underachiever, their chances of developing adult depression increase. This matters even more if bullying is done by multiple people rather than a single person. If the child is repeatedly punished without reason at school and if the parents have a cold attitude and don't listen to their child's version properly, the child often feels helpless and may suffer from depression during childhood itself.

Personality: Your partner for life

It is said that our personality or nature remains constant throughout our life. We all have distinct personalities, with our own set of strengths and shortcomings.

Depression is a state, meaning that it comes and goes. It may last for weeks or months, but most of the time, it is temporary. In contrast, personality implies a steady and predictable pattern of thinking, feeling, behaving and functioning, which stays with us more or less for a lifetime.

There are three major clusters of personality disorders. We all have certain shades of these clusters, but the majority of us don't have personality disorders. We think and behave as per our personality types, which are called 'personality traits'. Like some of us may have histrionic (attention-seeking) traits, but this won't be called a disorder as long as it doesn't cause difficulty in your day-to-day functioning or affect others. Let's look at these personalities in some detail.

Cluster A

People with cluster A personality disorders are generally seen as being odd and eccentric. Three further sub-types are common. The first one is schizoid personality disorder. These people are socially aloof, prefer solitary jobs and are happy being alone. Paranoid personality is the second variant. These people have mistrust and suspiciousness (paranoia) as their defining trait. They bear grudges for a longer time than most and have difficulty trusting people. The third variant in this type is schizotypal personality disorder, which is characterized by strikingly odd behaviour and thinking. Such people may have magical thinking, like relating two things in the mind which are completely unrelated, may have the feeling that other people are discussing them, and have vague speech, social anxiety and maybe even cult behaviour. All three personality types in cluster A do not necessarily have an increased risk of depression, but they have some risk of developing into schizophrenia.

Cluster B

People with cluster B personality disorders are quite prone to depression due to their relentless need for attention and importance in other people's eyes as well as for gaining approval or importance in matters beyond their control. In cluster B, we have four personality disorders. The first personality disorder is the most complex and challenging one: 'borderline personality disorder'. This personality type is on the borderline between neurosis (depression and anxiety) and psychosis (madness). It's characterized by extraordinarily unstable moods, instability in relationships, self-doubts, existential questions, chronic feelings of emptiness, anger dysregulation episodes, and multiple self-harm attempts such as slashing of wrists (which are not really serious suicide attempts), mostly done to gain attention and to get relief from psychological pain. They may be irritated at one moment, depressed at the next and feel normal immediately thereafter. The prevalence of depression in borderline personality disorders is quite high, up to 83 per cent.[11]

---

[11] Beatson, Josephine A. and Sathya Rao, 'Depression and borderline personality disorder', *The Medical Journal of Australia*, 29 October 2013, 199 (6): S24–S27, https://bit.ly/3CW9553. Accessed on 22 March 2022.

The second personality disorder is histrionic personality disorder. Unlike borderline personalities, people with this disorder don't have existential questions about themselves. They have high attention-seeking behaviour. They get uncomfortable in situations where they don't get attention, so they behave dramatically and try to gain attention both through physical appearance and style of speaking. As the need for attention may not be always fulfilled, they are prone to depression.

The third category in this cluster is narcissistic personality disorder. This is one step above histrionic personality disorder and is characterized by a sense of self-importance. People with this disorder have fantasies of unlimited success or power, consider themselves to be special, may exploit others for their needs, not value others and may be unempathetic towards others. They are more vulnerable to depression than common people, as they cannot handle life's blows or criticism due to their personality attributes.

The fourth personality disorder in this cluster is antisocial personality disorder, which is characterized by frequent criminal acts, deceitfulness, aggression, reckless disregard for the safety of others and a lack of remorse for hurting others and for their criminal acts. They are more prone to addictions and depression in old age.

Cluster C

The third personality disorder cluster is cluster C, which is characterized by high anxiety levels. In cluster C, we have three personality disorders. The first is avoidant personality disorder. People suffering from this generally avoid socialization due to fear of criticism, sensitivity to rejection and shyness. Avoidant personalities avoid socialization, but they differ from schizoid personalities in that they desperately want to socialize, while schizoid personalities are happy staying aloof. Their inferiority complex and fear of unacceptance prevent them from doing so.

The second type in this cluster is dependent personality disorder. As the name suggests, such people are always dependent on someone for major aspects of their lives. They lack confidence and have difficulty staying alone. In both dependent and avoidant personality disorder, patients' occupational functioning could be grossly impaired due to anxiety and the inability to work in a regular professional environment, which may, in turn, cause depression.

The third type in this cluster is obsessive-compulsive personality disorder, which is characterized by preoccupation with orderliness and perfectionism, and lack of flexibility and openness. For those suffering from this disorder, work always takes precedence over emotions. Also, they have difficulty spending money on themselves or on others. These people are again prone to later-life depression.

So, people with attention-seeking personalities, such as people who have histrionic personality disorder, narcissistic personality disorder or borderline personality disorder, are more prone to depression. As their primary pleasure principle is linked to 'attention and importance seeking', which is beyond their control, when they don't get it, it takes a toll on their self-esteem.

People with borderline personalities have an unstable temperament, chronic feelings of emptiness, anger dysregulation issues and questions about their identity. They are also prone to depression.

People with anxious avoidant personalities may suffer from depression and self-esteem issues, as internally they want to socialize and to be with people, but the fear of criticism, rejection and inadequacy always supervenes due to their intrinsic anxiety and inferiority complex, which are the part of their nature. The result is silent suffering.

One thing to note is that personality issues are difficult to address, as a person who has it often doesn't notice it themselves. When we say a personality is 'egosyntonic', it means that it is associated with the ego, and the person doesn't see that the problem lies in them. Second, it's very challenging to treat as it's the deep-seated mindset that defines a whole person.

The cigarette and the bottle

The most commonly seen disorder coexisting with alcoholism is depression. Almost 40–50 per cent cases of people with an alcohol addiction suffer from depression at some point in their life.[12] Now the cause-and-effect relationship differs from case to case. Alcohol can lead to depression and a clinically depressed person may get attracted to alcohol due to its temporary stress-relieving properties.

Alcohol initially increases the levels of serotonin and alters levels of dopamine in the body, which may result in temporary feelings of euphoria. However, in later stages, the levels of serotonin are reduced, causing depression. Also, alcohol is responsible for depression indirectly as it often causes family conflicts, job loss and other major medical issues. And once the patient understands they are dependent on alcohol, feelings of depression often increase.

Other substances like tobacco (nicotine), opioids (brown sugar) and cannabis (ganja) are often abused by depression patients, as they provide some relief by stimulating the happy

---

[12]Semple, David et al., *The Oxford Handbook of Psychiatry*, Oxford University Press, 2005.

pathways in the brain. But the majority of these substances cause depression in the long run by direct or indirect mechanisms once they become habitual.

One thing worth mentioning here is that addictions can be explained using a medical model, just like diabetes and hypertension. So, it's not entirely the patient's fault when they get addicted. Once we understand this, we stop blaming our relative or friend who suffers from addiction and instead try to help them get rid of it by medical means, just like any other disease.

Body affects the mind

Almost 50 per cent of brain stroke patients get depressed due to changes in the brain and the limitations caused by the stroke.[13] An almost similar percentage of depression is seen in patients affected by Parkinsonism. Various other neurological illnesses such as multiple sclerosis and motor neuron disease are common in depression.

Hypothyroidism (underactive thyroid) has a strong connection with depression, as good thyroid levels help in better neuronal communications and feelings of overall well-being. As much as 50 per cent of hypothyroid patients experience depression. In fact, earlier, thyroid hormones were used to treat resistant patients of depression.

Cancers may cause depression at the diagnosis and every stage of the treatment as well as when the patient relapses. The depression could be multifactorial—it could be caused by a big question mark that cancer has put to their future, the fear and anxiety at the suffering—with or without treatment,

---

[13]Ibid.

the tremendous expenditure involved in the cancer treatments, issues in the familial and social sphere, fear of disfigurement, loss of independence and losing the function of some of the body parts. It may even be caused by anger at God and be a side effect of a chemotherapeutic drug.

Other than this, various other diseases and infections like HIV, irritable bowel syndrome and inflammatory bowel diseases may cause depression, and their course is worsened by depression.

Deficiency of vitamin B12 and folic acid can increase the risk of depression and so can low haemoglobin levels.

Medicines used for managing hypertension, oral contraceptive pills, steroids and interferons can trigger depression in vulnerable patients.

Having other psychiatric illnesses is also a risk factor for depression. For example, half of the anxiety patients and almost 70 per cent of obsessive-compulsive disorder (OCD) patients have comorbid depression.[14] This depression happens when anxiety is untreated and the patient feels helpless over the primary psychiatric illness.

In psychotic disorders such as schizophrenia, the patient is depression-free only when they have full-blown schizophrenia, where insight is absent and the patient has an imaginary world of delusions and hallucinations. But patients develop depression when schizophrenia symptoms are brought under control and the they begin to understand the difference between what is real and what is unreal. After successful treatment, the patient understands how their life has been changed to a great extent due to schizophrenia, and this may lead to depression.

---

[14]Ibid.

Being a woman

Depression is two to three times more common in women than in men. There are multiple reasons for this. A few of them have been listed below as follows:

- The female brain is structurally different from the male brain. It is smaller in volume and has a bigger amygdala—the seat of emotions. This makes women more prone to depression.
- Hormones play a major role in regulating brain function. When oestrogen levels drop in the body, so do serotonin levels. This explains premenstrual syndrome and depression associated with it, as well as depression associated with post-partum period and perimenopausal period.
- Women face major challenges and new struggles in their life—right from puberty with their monthly cycles, then pregnancy, childbirths and lactation, right up to menopause. They have to manage several responsibilities while undergoing these as well. This creates a lot of stress, which makes them more prone to depression.
- Gender discrimination and the societal attitude have some role to play in this as well. Traditionally, a woman has to compromise a lot when it comes to her career and her wishes for the sake of the family. Even now, women's opinion is not valued in some strata of society. Malnutrition, domestic violence and sexual harassment are other challenges. Even in urban settings, many a time, the job profile and salary offered to them are not at par with that offered to their male counterparts.
- Women report depression more often, as they understand

their emotional states more clearly than men and have an attitude of seeking help for these. This explains the higher prevalence in women.

There are obviously some **protective factors** against depression, some of which are:

- A perceived good childhood
- A happy and healthy marital life
- Excellent self-esteem and a positive self-image
- Clarity on the goals of life
- High stress tolerance
- Good connect with the family
- Strong problem-solving skills
- A healthy lifestyle

Each of these and other factors too have been discussed in detail in the chapter on how to prevent depression.

The chemical source

Let's understand what exactly happens in the brain, the final and common pathway for all kinds of depression. It is popularly called the 'chemical locha'.

Two kinds of disturbances are possible in any organ of the body: structural and functional. In a structural disturbance, as the name itself suggests, we can find changes in the structure of that organ, such as changes in size or appearance, and it could be visible through various modalities of scanning. For example, in cases where we suspect pathology in the brain, a CT scan or an MRI scan is used. A functional disturbance means the changes may or may not be visible on structural imaging but are apparent in the organ's functioning. For example, one in four women have hypothyroidism. If you take an ultrasound scan of these women, majority of them will have normal results, but the thyroid will still not be functioning normally. For that, you would have to do a blood test, which assesses the functioning of the thyroid.

In depression as well, structural disturbances in the brain are not seen on brain imaging in all patients, although it is visible in patients with advanced and severe depressive features as changes in brain volume or enlargement of cavities (ventricles) of the brain. Some organs may even show a differential enhancement on these scans. But in mild cases of depression, these expensive tests are not recommended, nor is there any guarantee that we will see changes. More importantly, the scans do not change our line of treatment.

What we see on a functional scan like positron emission tomography (PET) is an altered brain metabolism in areas specific to depression. What actually happens in the brain at the neurochemical level, which cannot be seen in any scan, is altered levels of neurotransmitters. As a result, in chronic depression, we also see disturbed neural cell communication and brain cell loss. Many neurochemicals are affected in depression. One of the most severely affected, and one which causes the majority of the features of depression, is serotonin. It's the principal neurochemical responsible for the feeling of happiness, wellness, peace, self-esteem and social respect, and altered levels and altered functioning are the major causes of the plethora of symptoms of depression.

Along with this 'locha', altered levels of other chemicals can cause some other symptoms of depression. For example, lower levels of dopamine can make us feel less motivated, lethargic and may make a depressed person more prone to addiction. Altered levels of norepinephrine and gamma-aminobutyric acid

(GABA) can make a depressed person more sensitive to pain and lower the threshold of pain perception. This is the reason for multiple unexplained body pains perceived by a depressed person.

So, when a patient comes to us, as clinicians we have to understand the symptoms and the possible neurochemicals responsible for it and prescribe medicines accordingly such that they effectively address the underlying chemical pathology.

Demographics

The lifetime prevalence of depression worldwide is 15–20 per cent, and as per data shared by the WHO, globally more than 264 million people across all ages suffer from depression.[15] Also, unipolar depression was considered the second leading cause of the global disability burden in 2020.[16]

Gender prevalence: As stated earlier, it's two to three times more common in women.

Age group: Although no age group is immune to depression, almost 50 per cent of the patients of depression have the onset of the disorder between the ages 20 to 50.[17] The main reason for this is that these years see the maximum responsibility in terms of our life and of our dear ones. One has to face many struggles and cope with several challenges, such as building a career, taking

---

[15]Sadock, Benjamin James and Virginia Alcott Sadock, *Synopsis of Psychiatry*, 10th edition, Indian reprint, Lippincott Williams & Wilkins, 2007.

[16]Brooks, Megan, 'Depression Now World's Second Leading Cause of Disability', *Medscape*, 6 November 2013, https://wb.md/3thLOqV. Accessed on 17 March 2022.

[17]Sadock, Benjamin James and Virginia Alcott Sadock, *Synopsis of Psychiatry*, 10th edition, Indian reprint, Lippincott Williams & Wilkins, 2007.

some risks and making relevant decisions, digesting rejections at the personal and professional fronts, getting married, adjusting with the spouse and planning and starting a new family, taking care of children, planning finances, buying property, building a reputation and credibility in our respective domains, and taking care of ageing parents. The journey through each of these may not be smooth for everyone and may thus lead to breakdowns. This is why the prevalence of depression is highest in this age group.

Old age: Almost 10–20 per cent of the elderly suffer from depression in India, although the prevalence could be even more as most of the time it is underreported by patients and not clearly understood by relatives.[18] Also, it presents non-classical symptoms such as body pains, irritability, confusion, etc. The contributory causes of depression in this age are physical illnesses in almost two-thirds of the cases, loss of spouse, lack of trustworthy and supportive relationships, loneliness, adjustment issues with new family members or caretaker, and fear of getting dependent and impending death.

Childhood and teenage: Various studies in India have reported the prevalence of depression in children to be 2–20 per cent.[19] According to the *Indian Journal of Psychiatry* 2019, almost 50 million children are found to be going through some mental health issues and more than two-thirds of them do not seek help. And as per the survey reported in *The State of the World's Children 2021* almost one in seven adolescents reported feeling depressed,

---

[18] Barua, Ankur et al., 'Prevalence of depressive disorders in the elderly', *Annals of Saudi Medicine*, November–December 2011, 31(6): 620–24, https://bit.ly/3KMT5VK. Accessed on 17 March 2022.

[19] Grover, Sandeep et al., 'Depression in Children and Adolescents: A Review of Indian studies', *Indian Journal of Psychological Medicine*, May–June 2019; 41(3): 216–27, https://bit.ly/3tht6jh. Accessed on 17 March 2022.

amounting to prevalence of almost 14 per cent in adolescents.[20]

There could be several reasons for depression in children, such as adjustment issues, poor scholastic performance, different forms of abuse, bullying, lack of support from peers and the emotional unavailability of parents.

In teens, in addition to the factors mentioned in childhood depression, gadget addiction, addiction to other substances, rejection and bullying by peers and negative self-image are important contributory factors.

Socio-economic class: Although depression is commonly seen in all socio-economic classes, the prevalence is a little higher in the lower socio-economic strata. The main reasons cited in various studies are poverty, difficulty in meeting basic needs, fewer opportunities for recreation, overcrowding at home, poor living conditions and less privacy.[21]

Urban lifestyle: The rates of various mental illnesses are quite high in cities. According to various meta-analyses conducted between 2000 and 2010 and a detailed paper published in *Nature* in 2011, cities are associated with higher rates of mental health problems as compared with a rural set-up—almost 40 per cent higher risk of depression, over 20 per cent more risk of anxiety and much higher rates of loneliness, isolation and stress.[22] The

---

[20] 'UNICEF report spotlights on the mental health impact of COVID-19 in children and young people', UNICEF India, 5 October 2021, https://uni.cf/3CWkRfJ. Accessed on 17 March 2022.

[21] Freeman, Aislinne et al., 'The role of socio-economic status in depression: results from the COURAGE (aging survey in Europe)', *BMC Public Health*, 19 October 2016, https://bit.ly/3IhWgD6. Accessed on 17 March 2022.

[22] Lederbogen, Florian et al., 'City living and urban upbringing affect neural social stress processing in humans', *Nature*, 474, 498–501 (2011), 22 June 2011, https://go.nature.com/3th6gbo. Accessed on 17 March 2022; Kennedy,

contributory causes of this difference are exhausting schedules, long commutes, less time for recreation and family, disturbed lifestyle, sleep disturbances, less time for taking rest, a feeling of losing touch with the roots of our culture, less communal support, less time for making meaningful friendships, seeking gratification in short-standing relationships which in turn bring more stress, financial tensions, job insecurities, overcrowding, daily issues with varieties of pollution, overexposure to loud noise, constant honking on the roads, newer construction noises, exposure to bright light and virtual fatigue.

All these stimuli affect brain chemistry as well. According to a study published in *Nature* in 2011[23] on how city life brings about changes in neural social stress processing, it was found on the functional imaging of the brain of volunteers that the amygdala was hyperfunctioning and another area of the brain— the cingulate cortex, which responds to negative emotional stress—was also found to be affected in those raised in urban set-ups. The details are discussed in the chapter on urban depression.

When we read the demographics and prevalence of depression, we need to keep this in mind—what we are seeing is probably not the representative picture of depression as it's often underrecognized and underreported.

Daniel P. and Ralph Adolphs, 'Stress and the city', *Nature,* 474, 452–53 (2011), 22 June 2011, https://go.nature.com/3Im38PQ. Accessed on 17 March 2022.
[23]Ibid.

3
MY WOES IN THE CITY

Let's do this simple exercise. Close your eyes and imagine two scenarios.

The first is of city life, where you have a job that involves a long commute, pressures to meet deadlines on most days, a life where you are struggling for existence, struggling with insecurity, envy and jealousy, having the constant fear of being fired, and struggling for promotions and incentives. You compensate for your week on the weekends, when you lie for long hours in a big comfortable bed, go for outings in posh, big malls and have meals in restaurants with an awesome ambience or order in food. On some weekends, you meet up with friends, but that too after deciding a few weeks prior, it is never impromptu. Most of the time new friendships feel superficial and rarely do you feel like you are talking to friends who are genuinely concerned. You don't have time for family other than on weekends. Communication within the family on those off days also seems difficult, as the majority of arguments happen on those two days because of the pent-up stress of the weekdays and the dissatisfaction in various domains of life. You have difficulty taking time out for exercise and for your hobbies. As the years pass, your income keeps growing but so do your needs—your need for financial management and the need to maintain your social position. This appears to be an unending tryst and the feelings of having 'lost the real me' dominate your mind space.

In the second scenario, you're living in a small city, working in a nine-to-five job, where you may not be making as much money. But you have to commute less and have the time to enjoy with family, even with your extended family. You can take out time to visit theatres and enjoy listening to music. You have a cozy circle of friends, whom you can visit anytime, where people know you and you know many beyond professional reasons. Everything you want and love is in and around your vicinity. You feel connected with your roots and with yourself too. There is less screentime and more face time. You may not go to big malls for outings but maybe to a friend's place or to nearby gardens and parks. You may not be visiting posh five-star restaurants, but small local eateries instead. People around you may not have polished communication skills but they talk genuinely—from the heart, celebrate with you in good times and hold your hand during rough patches, where love compensates for all inconveniences.

If given an option, which scenario would you opt for? Many of us would choose the second scenario.

Priorities differ from person to person. Undoubtedly, city life offers more opportunities, more chances for fulfilling our dreams, a more sophisticated life and a better civic culture, but these come at a big cost, as we saw in the first scenario. Many get disillusioned once they start living in a big city with the compromises and struggles it involves, but they continue to dwell in the city given the demand of their work life. They have no choice. But given an option, many would opt for the second scenario, as with age, what most of us want is a stable, quiet and productive life without much hustle-bustle and struggle.

Let's go through a few cases in urban settings which could be suggestive of depression in different age groups.

Pain behind my anger

Tara, a 14-year-old girl, was brought by her parents to our OPD. She was feeling increased irritability, showing adamant behaviour with her parents and spending excessive time on gadgets. When at home, she always kept the door of her room locked. She was suffering from disturbed sleep, showing poor scholastic performance and spending excessively, but was unable to explain why this was happening. She had become secretive too. Most of the time she did not allow her parents to enter her room. If she was forced to keep the door of her room open, she would shout at them and start crying immediately after that. Then there were periods when she didn't talk to them for days. Her parents found her drawings of a skeleton, needles and a hanging girl. She was blaming her parents for some old incidents that happened in early childhood. She was showing these symptoms for almost six months when she was brought to the OPD.

On enquiry, we found that the child had been born after a full-term, normal delivery. She started walking and talking at the expected age and had had no major illness. Since both parents were working, she was raised in an after-school day-care for several years. She was also getting trained in classical music and basketball till the previous year, which she had discontinued. She had been an above-average performer at school till the previous year, but her performance had gone down over the last few months.

When we spoke to the child, we found that she was feeling low and lonely more or less all the time. She was not interested in the majority of her activities except for social media. She said she was using this mainly as a diversion from the low and disturbing thoughts, and it had now become a compulsion for her. She had difficulty in focusing, had low motivation and felt like sitting idle most of the time. She was mostly anxious and felt better only when she got a specific number of likes on her social media posts and at least 10 new followers a week. She had very few friends but had recently tried to socialize more because of her loneliness. She had tried cannabis multiple times because she thought it would make her feel better, but in fact, she faced more mood swings after that. She had difficulty in falling asleep and maintaining sleep. She also had disturbed appetite and low energy levels. She said she was a loner since childhood as she was an only child and both her parents were working in a nuclear family set-up. She held her parents responsible for her mood swings, as they did not understand her. She always felt their absence in her childhood, and they engaged her in some hobby class or other as they did not have time for her. She got attracted and attached to boys quickly, as it made her feel secure. She liked the attention, but she was often disinterested in physical intimacy. She felt her life was an overall failure and tried to seek approval on social media to lessen those feelings. She was unable to share lots of things with her parents now as she didn't feel a bond with them. Their concern and constant enquiries felt like an intrusion to her. Their attitude seemed accusatory. Since she had trouble adjusting with everyone around her, like her friends and family, they thought *she* was the problem. This further annoyed her. Her parents mainly brought her to me for her behavioural issues such as aggression and irritability. In reality, what this early teenager was going through was agitated depression.

Although the majority of teenagers go through periods of rebellion and distantiation from their parents as a part of normal adolescence, this was clearly in excess as the depression was overpowering her day-to-day activities and she was gradually losing confidence. She was treated with medications to get her out of her depression, and reduce her impulsivity and preoccupation with the same thoughts. Once better, she was put on psychotherapy to correct her thought distortions. Family therapy was also given to all three of them together.

Although this is not the story of all teenagers in the city, many go through these problems while growing up in metros. What are the solutions for this? How do we give quality time to our child when living in a nuclear family without the support of grandparents or close relatives? How do we keep the parent–child bond strong and healthy? Some parenting tips, especially for the growing teens, on how to keep a check on their gadgets use, how to use technology for strengthening rather than breaking the parent–child bond and how to identify the deviation from normalcy in the child are described in the chapter dealing with special situations in urban life.

Back to my roots

Shubham, a 20-year-old young man, came to me once. He had faced an anxiety attack when he was undergoing an MRI for pain in the elbow a month back. What occurred was a panic attack due to the closed space and the loud sound of the MRI machine. He had palpitations, breathlessness, an impending sense of doom and death and a few other symptoms. When it settled, he thought he was overthinking issues as he was stressed because of multiple reasons for the last 18 months. His current job was not very rewarding—he felt underpaid, underrecognized and often criticized for not being able to meet deadlines. Whenever he tried to clear his doubts, he was humiliated and his questions were not answered properly by his seniors. He was unclear about his job role and was having difficulty focusing and motivating himself to work. He could not even think of leaving the job as he had family responsibilities. He wanted to pursue higher education abroad but was afraid to go ahead with it, as it would exhaust his savings.

Due to these pressures, he often felt trapped, suffocated and unable to escape the current situation. He was staying as a paying guest quite far from his workplace—he could not afford to stay nearer as the office was in the IT park and all accommodations were very expensive in that area. The commute took around 90 minutes one way, and he travelled every day in the office bus. He had to get up at 6 a.m. to catch the office bus at 7 a.m. He was not even getting seven hours of sleep on most weekdays as meetings and work often extended till late at night. He had difficulties falling asleep and often woke up feeling all the more tired. He even tried to talk to his colleagues about the situation, but they were always too occupied. He felt that his family members would not understand his situation and would end up getting more stressed. Lately he was getting affected by minor physical discomforts and was concerned that if something major happened to him, there was no one to take care of his responsibilities. Most of the time, he was engaged in a vicious cycle of negative thoughts about the future, particularly regarding his job and health.

He had lost interest in the activities he enjoyed earlier, like watching movies and going out. His food habits were erratic—he overate when stressed and had gained 10 kilograms in the previous year, making him feel sluggish and tired most of the time. Although his family members wanted him to settle down, he felt the future was bleak with his current job and salary. He also felt the amount of time he was committing to the current job was far more than what he was paid. He avoided social media, as others' posts made him feel all the more bad about himself and his life. He often felt there was no reason to live in the city other than his job. He wanted a life that wasn't so taxing and in which he would find a better connect with himself and others.

Outwardly, these symptoms hinted at a quarter-life crisis, which happens around the age of 25. At this stage, a person has to go through multiple stressors and demands of life, like taking major career decisions, settling financially, looking after ageing parents and starting their own family. This is a 'normative crisis', meaning that most of the people face it without getting majorly affected in any domain of life. But sometimes, some young adults go through depression, as in this case, where he is losing all hope for the future and has ideas of helplessness, and low moods and low energy levels are his constant companions. Depression in such cases is more common when a person is staying in metros, away from the family's warmth, working in highly exhausting schedules with lower payment than expected and lacking communal support. Many of them feel trapped in this situation, as only metros offer a scope of a career in their chosen field. They have to stay and adjust to this way of life come what may and cannot go back to their home town.

A study conducted by the Associated Chambers of Commerce and Industry of India (ASSOCHAM) showed that 42.5 per cent of employees in the Indian private sector are afflicted with general anxiety disorder or depression as compared with government employees.[24] This is attributed to lower pay and longer working hours, which contributes to an atmosphere of constant fatigue that further develops into stress and frustration, thereby acutely affecting mental health. India has become the

---

[24]Joshi, Pallavi, 'World Mental Health Day: Nearly half of India Inc employees suffer from depression', *The Economic Times*, 10 October 2018, https://bit.ly/3MYbGjy. Accessed on 17 March 2022.

hub of 'cheap labour' for most of the employers across the globe.

A private-sector employee in India works for a minimum of 48–50 hours a week when compared with 33 hours a week in the UK and 40 hours a week in the US. Also, the pay scale in India, a developing country, is meagre when compared with developed countries, which pay almost six times more even after deducting the indexing prices and cost of living.[25] This leads to extremely demanding schedules, elevated stress levels and performance pressure. Thus, in a bid to aid and add to the 'cheap labour' of the corporate industry, the Indian working class has traded its peace of mind and leisure.

According to the same study, clinical depression has risen by around 50 per cent in the last eight years, which, in turn, results in an array of multifarious ailments that are gradually creeping in. As much as 23 per cent of the private-sector employees are afflicted by obesity due to their poor work–life balance and a sedentary lifestyle.[26] Often food is abused as an antidepressant as it's easy to access and may come to your rescue as a stress buster, which, in turn, augments the threat of diabetes, hypertension and cardiac disorders. Clinical depression is a highly sensitive matter. Belittling it in anyway could even turn fatal.

Not everyone can opt for the small city life and neither can they avoid the stressors completely. But everyone can surely build the resilience for combating stress and preventing depression.

---

[25] Salgaonkar, Hitesh, 'A Study on the Role of Organisation in Ensuring Mental and Physical Health of Employees', *Scribd*, https://bit.ly/3Im9TRI. Accessed on 17 March 2022.

[26] Joshi, Pallavi, 'World Mental Health Day: Nearly half of India Inc employees suffer from depression', *The Economic Times*, 10 October 2018, https://bit.ly/3MYbGjy. Accessed on 17 March 2022.

I don't want to go back

Sunil, a 50-year-old gentleman, came to us for marital therapy. As a protocol of marital therapy, we first evaluate both partners to find out if they have any mental health issues. If it's found, we treat that first and begin the therapy only once the illness is under control.

The man was working as the chief operating officer (COO) for a big corporate company. He was facing issues related to marriage. Although he was grateful for the sacrifices his wife made in the initial years of their marriage, over the years both of them had evolved in different directions and shared nothing in common except their 16-year-old son. He was having an extramarital affair for the last two years, and before that he had had a fling with a colleague too. His wife came to know about this a month back. His wife had become more of a room-mate, and their relationship was devoid of any physical intimacy. He said he was not attracted to her any more and felt it was a pressure to get intimate if she asked for it. Sharing between them had become minimal, as he returned home quite late due to long working hours. On weekends, he preferred to sleep for long hours or opted to go out with friends instead of spending time at home, with his family. Lately his subordinates were giving him trouble and repeatedly complaining about his rough attitude. He was consuming two cans of beer almost every day for the last couple of years to feel relaxed and get good sleep. About the extramarital affair, he said it was out of pure physical attraction and there were no strings attached. Meeting his girlfriend helped him relax. Now, even though the wife was in the know about it, he was not too keen to end the affair.

He also said he was going through a turmoil, as the atmosphere at the home front and at the office was not good.

He didn't have the energy to start anything new in his career. His energy levels were steadily dipping and his life was largely mechanical. He claimed a great attachment to his son, who was currently studying in Class XII. He said his girlfriend and the drinks were the only two things helping him in the current gloomy situation.

When we spoke to the wife, she said she felt betrayed after she came to know about her husband's affair. It came as a big shock. She had compromised a lot, even given up her career after childbirth. In the initial years after childbirth, she was left with no time for her husband but later she tried to compensate for that. He however gradually lost interest and now they hardly interacted. She desperately wanted to work on their marriage. It took her several weeks to come to terms with his affair, but had now moved on from anger and hurt to acceptance. She had an issue with his unapologetic attitude about the affair and in general as well. In all these years, his ego had become difficult to handle, and after every argument and fight, it was she who was apologizing. She now wanted some remedy for his tyrannical behaviour as a part of marital therapy.

This case is quite common in an urban setting. Midlife is a challenging period for most men and women—it's the time where hormones go for a toss in both genders, and most marriages typically have some issues that have accumulated over the years. Sometimes both partners evolve in different directions, which may happen if they don't spend enough time with each other due to busy schedules and other responsibilities. Also, it's difficult to remain attracted to the changing (read ageing) body of the partner. Continuing physical intimacy can be challenging because of all these issues.

Most people come out of the midlife crisis without much damage to their relationships or they work with a gradual acceptance of this inevitable developmental crisis. They also get more insight into life being limited and that ageing, which is inevitable, has begun. In some cases, especially in metros, where schedules are very busy and very little time is spent with the family, work is given supreme importance till middle age and less time is spent on other hobbies and in developing other domains. That's why chances of depression are higher. Most extramarital affairs happen during this period, possibly due to a lack of attraction towards the spouse and increasing frustration in the career. For many, career wise, a certain amount of monotony sets in and the desire to learn anything new or to change the career path is practically absent. Affairs add spice to life or provide a reassurance that they are still attractive. Extramarital affairs invariably bring more trouble in their already troubled lives and can even have a devastating impact on the lives of those involved. Impulsive indulgence in alcohol and detachment with the family may happen with some people.

Another frequent scenario which we come across in people of this age is that men in their 40s suffer from intolerable anxiety and anger, often after their wives are caught having an affair with someone in their known circle. This is often discovered by teenaged children or by themselves through some suspicious messages. When the wife admits to having an affair after a confrontation, the situation at home becomes intolerable, with initial threats of breaking the marriage. Then comes acceptance, with frequent outbursts of anger due to the betrayal. Sometimes, the man forces his wife to reveal more information about the affair, particularly the extent of physical involvement. This may lead to greater intimacy from the husband, as unconsciously they feel that the betrayal was a consequence of a lack of physical satisfaction and underperformance at their end.

In such cases, the woman often complains that her husband

works very long hours and goes on tours often, resulting in less communication and appreciation and more criticism. This results in a dysfunctional relationship. Living in a nuclear family with grown-up children who remain outside the house most of the time also contributes to her loneliness. Nowadays, social media provides much more opportunity for meeting other people. Most of the time, it begins with someone giving extra attention to her status on social media. This slowly increases to complimenting the woman for simple things. Many a time, because of the void that they perceive in the marriage, women get attracted to the attention given by other men. The real challenge is when the woman has to concede to her partner's unrealistic expectations at the cost of her family time, leading to a feeling of guilt and remorse. If she refuses, sometimes the partner threatens to make the affair public or to inform her family. In the process of concealing the affair, one or more family members might get the hint. Besides, living a dual life is always difficult. Negative self-image and public image become more difficult to handle, more so when infidelity exposes the woman. Societal attitudes towards female infidelity are still harsh, and the outcome of an extramarital relationship is often not taken into consideration by women when they casually start it. This entire situation may worsen the stress and depression in many cases.

Addressing these issues involve building a positive self-image, setting the right goals and establishing assertive communication in addition to marital therapy and treatment for the depression. All of these are discussed in detail in subsequent chapters.

My home doesn't shift

Aruna, a 68-year-old woman, was referred to us by her physician for multiple pains in the body and on-and-off anxiety symptoms for the last seven months. Symptoms started almost a month after the death of her husband and had worsened progressively. She was brought to her son's place in a bigger city immediately after the death of her spouse as there was nobody to look after her in her home town.

When we spoke with Aruna, she said that she did not feel at peace over here. She felt her home was a much better place, where she had spent most of her life. She felt lonely over here, anxious when she was alone in the room. She felt weak and had low-intensity pain all over her body. She said that life over here was fast, and she wouldn't be able to cope with it. She was getting overwhelmed with simple tasks like going out for a walk. The fast life of her children and grandchildren, their constant movement in and out of the house, the cook arriving at 6 a.m.— all of these were acting as triggers. She missed the relaxed life of her home town. She tried to make friends with women her age whom she met during the evening strolls, but she faced a language barrier. Progressive loss of hearing was a major hindrance in communicating with others. She felt totally dependent on her son for all small and big needs. She missed her husband a lot and missed companionship in her life even more. Adjusting to this place and pace seemed very difficult.

Although for every household task there was help, she didn't feel comfortable. The only time she felt better was when her son and daughter-in-law spent time with her, along with her grandchildren, which usually happened on weekends. She also enjoyed watching some of her favourite television serials in her mother tongue. She had lost interest in other activities, such as chanting, cooking, etc. She found it difficult to sleep and would get up in the middle of night multiple times to use the washroom and then struggled to go back to sleep. She would spend most of the day in bed.

She would constantly compare her current life with what she had before in her home town, where she was surrounded by relatives and had strong communal support. Her life there was at an easier pace, with no hurries. She missed that simple life and the freedom.

Depression in the elderly in an urban set-up is a common occurrence in clinical practice, particularly when elderly people shift to a bigger city following the death of their spouse or to look after their grandchildren, leaving their home town, where they have spent most of their life. Although they don't have to take care of the usual household chores, they often feel anxious at not being able to cope with the speed of city life. They feel lonely and miss the communal support which small cities offer. Depression in elderly patients usually comes with changes in personality, anxiety, multiple body pains and drastic changes in their routine.

How to deal with late-life challenges and depression is discussed in the next chapter, but in such cases, management revolves around treating depression, encouraging socializing, respecting their independence, security and financial needs, involving them in routine activities, setting small and achievable goals for them and addressing their concerns and anxiety about their current and future life.

Already in my heart

Niharika, a 35-year-old woman, visited us after a failed in-vitro fertilization (IVF) cycle. She was getting repeated bouts of crying and a sense of purposelessness and emptiness after this recent failure.

On further enquiry, we found that she had a late marriage due to educational commitments as well as a demanding career.

She took longer to find a suitable alliance because her career was a priority and there was a time crunch. She had got married at the age of 32. The couple tried to have a baby since the start of their marriage, and had started taking treatment under the fertility consultant. The current issue she was facing was that there was very little time for intimacy. Since the start of the fertility treatment, it had become even more stressful. Sometimes she was even questioning the purpose of the intimacy as it did not help with conception. Communication with her husband had also reduced. She had to take leaves from her demanding job for fertility treatments, which was adding to the stress. She had to postpone all her holiday plans.

She started avoiding social functions in her home town, as she would inevitably be bombarded with questions regarding her plan to have kids. It was also difficult for her to deal with the fact that most of her friends were already parents. She would get disturbed by the news of any of her close relatives getting pregnant. While she was happy for them, it only made her realize her unfulfilled wish all the more. As her husband's test reports were fine, she felt guilty about him suffering because of her reduced fertility. She felt stressed a week before the pregnancy test and had difficulty in performing routine tasks. When the test was negative (as it had been so far), she felt terrible for the next couple of days, after which she tried to slowly resume her routine. The recent IVF cycle further aggravated her mood swings, possibly due to painful treatments and hormone injections as well as high hopes that did not materialize.

Although infertility is not exclusively a problem of an urban set-up, it's more common in cities as the age of marriage is often advanced. Adjustment with the spouse takes longer. Intimacy and communication issues due to busy schedules are common. The constant stress may lead to hormonal disturbances in both partners, increasing chances of infertility further, which, in turn, adds more stress to the relationship.

How to regulate stress during this period, how to keep relationship with the spouse smooth and how certain important decisions may be required in the course of treatment are some of the factors discussed in detail in the next chapter.

Work till I drop

Vinod, a 40-year-old male doctor who works as a neurosurgeon in a big corporate hospital, suffered a massive heart attack and required angioplasty and extracorporeal membrane oxygenation (ECMO) for a few days. Once he was ready to be discharged, he was referred to us. He was not obese, didn't have diabetes or hypertension, was taking the stairs instead of the elevator every day in the hospital and was eating healthy food. In other words, he had none of the standard risk factors associated with heart attack. Except one—he was sleepless every other night due to hospital calls after his OPD and operation theatre (OT) hours. He was under tremendous stress due to work and family commitments. He was working roughly 12–15 hours a day and was attending emergency calls every alternate Sunday. It had taken him several years to get the position of consultant in this big corporate hospital and so did not want to put the financial stability at stake. Although attending night calls was nothing new for him, of late he had been complaining of mild chest pain. He thought this was a result of bloating and acidity, which he often got because of his hectic work schedule and lack of sleep.

When asked about his mood before the heart attack, he said he was not getting the time to understand what he was feeling, hence could not comment on it. All he remembered was just rushing to the hospital all days of the week and most of the nights, trying to keep his calm in difficult situations such as urgent brain surgeries and explaining the gravity of the situation to relatives and patients. He felt emotionally broken after the heart attack, and thinking about the future made him even more anxious. He said, 'In this medical field, I have to work hard, as there are no fixed hours and with this morbidity, I am not even sure if I will be able to stand and work for several hours in the OPD and OT. How will I manage further?' He had anticipated and prepared himself for problems that might crop up in the future, but this was really unforeseen and had shaken him.

Many doctors and others living extremely busy and hectic lives in metros are prone to major illnesses; this is a well-studied topic. Particularly in the medical field, on an average, 10–15 years are spent in studying the subject and becoming an expert, from getting admission into an MBBS course, passing yearly exams and doing an internship, to preparing for the postgraduate entrance exam, doing a super-speciality course and finally settling in some big hospital as a consultant with a lucrative salary. But even after becoming a consultant, it's not a nine-to-five job for most of the clinical branches, especially in surgical. They have to manage OPD and OT duties and be on call duties, adding to the stress.

Stress affects all organs in the body, not just the mind. Long-term stress paralyses the psycho-neuro-immune system, and a high amount of inflammatory cytokines are released in the body, which makes it prone to all kinds of illnesses, infectious as well as non-infectious. All major diseases have a strong causal association with stress. Stress ages the blood vessels faster and makes them harder, increases blood pressure and the chances of stroke, causes rhythm disturbances in the heart, elevates blood sugar, reduces the count and functions of natural killer cells and hastens the process of carcinogenesis (cancer formation) in susceptible individuals. Stress also reduces immunity and makes a person susceptible to infections in the long run. For the mind, the 'fight and flight' cycle caused by the hormone adrenaline is actually a protective response when it is triggered at the right time and it prepares the individual from impending danger by making the mind more alert, increasing the heart rate, dilating the pupils, etc. But if this alarm of fight-and-flight reaction keeps buzzing all the time without any actual danger to life, what will it cause in the long run? Breakdown in the mind and body too, right? This stress can lead to fatigue, sleep disturbances, lower performance, easy fatiguability, anger dysregulation issues, depression and anxiety in the long run.

It's not easy to handle a stressful lifestyle, surely not after a particular age. Up to a certain age, the mind and body can handle any degree of hard work: as said correctly, in youth, we can even digest a stone if swallowed by mistake! But as age advances, resilience of both body and mind reduces, and we need to rebuild it with the right lifestyle, right thinking and taking 'pauses' at the right time. These things are addressed in detail in the chapter on how to build resilience.

I need a companion

Ramani, a 33-year-old female patient, was referred to us by her treating physician after a recent suicide attempt. She was a banker and had had quite a stable job for a few years. She said she was facing issues with her current relationship—she was not sure if the guy had broken up with her. She had been in multiple relationships in the last four years, all through matrimonial and dating websites, but all were short lived, including this one.

The typical pattern she noticed was that men took interest

in her and she got involved quickly, aiming for a long-term commitment every time. She was disappointed whenever she spoke about her intention to get married. Her parents, who lived in a different city, were unaware of the details of her involvement with these men, and they were also trying at their levels to seek alliances for her through friends and relatives. Most of her friends were happily married and settled. Talking to her parents and friends about the challenges she was facing was also getting difficult. She was afraid of being judged for her multiple flings. Every rejection and break-up was a blow to her self-confidence, and she had started questioning her own worth. Of late, the thought of meeting prospective alliances petrified her.

Although her work life was going well, two of her ex-boyfriends happened to be her colleagues, and every time she saw them at work, the bitterness of the break-ups crept in on her. She had lost faith in relationships but at the same time was desperately seeking a life partner. She even thought of moving in with her parents, as it would be easier for her to gauge the wedding proposals. However, the taunts of visiting relatives haunted her. Besides, she was habituated to living independently.

Sometimes she missed the innocence she had a few years back. In between the serious relationships, she had gone for casual dates to break the cycle of loneliness, but she found them superficial now.

Longing for companionship and the onset of loneliness are common occurrences in urban life. Usually while treating such cases, in addition to treating depression, developing a support system, a better connection with the self and a better self-image forms the cornerstone. Next come identifying repetitive maladaptive patterns in the relationship, if any, and correcting them for better future relationships.

Life in a metro

A wonderful movie came out a few years back called *Life in a Metro* which had a strong and captivating storyline and threw light on various factors in urban life that lead to depression.

Sharman Joshi plays the character of a boy from a small town with the dream of constructing a big bungalow. This is actually the dream of his late father, who never makes enough money to actualize that dream. Joshi's character starts lending his flat for a few hours in rotation to his colleagues and bosses for their hook-ups, in exchange for monetary benefits and to gain early promotion. He suffers from loneliness and is even heartbroken when he comes to know the girl he secretly likes is having an affair with his boss.

K.K. Menon essays the role of a workaholic boss who has suffered distantiation from his wife (played by Shilpa Shetty) in the course of their marriage. He feels his wife keeps nagging all the time, as a result of which he starts opting for transient and convenient relationships with some of his colleagues.

In the movie, Shilpa Shetty is a stay-at-home mom by choice, someone who has given up her career to raise their daughter. She struggles to live in a loveless and respectless marriage. They often have house parties to keep communication alive.

Shiny Ahuja is a struggling stage artist who has a lot of talent but is financially unstable. As a result, his spouse leaves him. Underappreciation and underrecognition for his talent form the basis of his depression. Living a lonely life, he tries to find a companion in Shilpa (K.K. Menon's wife), where they have emotionally intimate moments. But the relationship doesn't go beyond that, as Shilpa finds it difficult to break the marital bond and settle with him abroad.

Konkana Sen Sharma is shown as a woman in her early 30s

who is desperately looking for a life partner to settle down with. Given her educational commitments, she finds she has become little old for marriage. She says she often eats lots of chocolates but that doesn't help with her depression. In desperation, she has a fling with a gay colleague, who just uses her to show his overbearing parents that he has a girlfriend. It comes as a shock when she finds out about this and goes into depression. Irrfan Khan then comes to her rescue, giving her a different perspective on life. They eventually end up getting married.

Kangana Ranaut, who is shown sharing an accommodation with Konkana Sen, carries the trauma of past relationships and the guilt of having an affair with her room-mate's brother-in-law (K.K. Menon). When Kangana questions him about the relationship and their future, he lashes out on her. Traumatized, she attempts suicide. Sharman Joshi saves her and they get closer.

Dharmendra and Nafisa Ali are shown as old lovers. Dharmendra comes to meet her after a gap of 40 years. Dharmendra had left her to pursue his dreams abroad, while Nafisa got married. Her husband passed away sometime back and her children live abroad. She is shown as living in an old-age home, leading a normal life. Both of them are delighted to meet each other again. Her children, who put her in the old-age home, disapprove of the relationship, but both of them continue to meet despite that. Eventually, Nafisa peacefully dies in Dharmendra's arms, who later says that some shortcuts in life actually tend to become very long routes, meaning that he left her without any notice for the big opportunity, which actually blocked his personal share of fulfilling experiences. It took him a long time and immense courage to come back and pursue what he actually wanted.

What is common between all the characters in this

movie? Dissatisfaction with life. Except for Irrfan Khan, all the characters are depressed and lonely, and they adopt bad coping mechanisms. Many of them are living in the past, have financial issues and struggle for existence. Their extramarital relations stem not out of love but out of an unsatisfactory and dysfunctional marriage, and they face the same issues with their new partner. They have less time for productive relationships and make compromises with their existing partners and their job. They attempt to 'find' themselves in disruptive behaviours, thus facing moral dilemmas in the process. They face the heavy cost of guilt from their actions.

Probably this is the story of many who struggle in urban life. This surely doesn't mean we need to leave this urban set-up and live in semi-urban or village settlements, as city life has different advantages. As per the prediction of the United Nations (UN), 70 per cent of the world's population will be staying in cities by 2030.[27] But an awareness of the challenges can help in acknowledging the early signs of distress, and timely building of resilience can save a lot of suffering.

---

[27] '70% of the World's Population Will Live in Cities by 2030, While 60% of Urban Settlements Remain to be Built (UN-Habitat, World Cities Report)', World Water Council, https://bit.ly/3thUi1t. Accessed on 17 March 2022.

4
CRISES IN MY LIFE

Situations like a break-up, marital discord, parenting issues, problems of the elderly, infertility, post-partum blues, examination stress, death of loved ones, orientation issues and job losses exist in the rural set-up too, but their prevalence is much higher in an urban set-up. Rural life has many shock absorbers which are absent in city life, such as an easy paced life, communal support, less struggle to meet day-to-day needs, and more time for friendships and recreation. The impact of these events is more pronounced in an urban setting, and if addressed properly, the distress caused can be halted at the right time and won't pose a risk for depression.

Break-Up

Some of the most regular visitors to our OPD are aged between 16 and 35, looking a little dishevelled. Our conversation usually goes something like this.

'I don't know why I am here, Doctor, but I am very disturbed.'
'What happened?'
(*sobbing*) 'Where should I start? I am not getting any sleep. I'm unable to focus, and I am irritated all the time.'
'Any tension you are facing lately?'
(*sobs again*)

'Financial issues? Any professional tensions?'
'No, no, I can handle those.'
'Okay, are there any relationship issues?'
'Yes!'

This is a typical profile of a person who has recently had a break-up, and this is our initial routine conversation. The younger generation usually digests the rest of the stressors well, but this 'punch' is difficult to deal with. It is correctly said that in a relationship, you can show your best side as well as your worst. People behave irrationally after a break-up because they feel humiliated. They may get addicted to illicit substances and go into depression. A lot of time—time which is very precious at this age—is wasted in this process.

To avoid these complications, depression and other mental health problems, we can do a few things, which are discussed below.

Before the actual break-up, the relationship undergoes immense change. This is because either one or both partners start distancing themselves from each other much earlier and may in fact get a sense of the impending break-up. The approval of two people is essential for a relationship to continue, but for a break-up, even one person's decision is enough. Therein lies the problem.

Here are a few cautions and unwritten norms that we should follow during a break-up.

If you are the one looking to end the relationship, please talk to your partner face to face about it. WhatsApp, Facebook or Instagram are not the right mediums for it. Don't declare such decisions over the phone either. Meeting the other person is always advisable. It's always better to explain the reasons behind your break-up because if a person doesn't know the reasons, then the question lingers and leads to many misunderstandings.

After all, everyone deserves an explanation and a closure to move on in life. You can handle the situation in a mature way without personally attacking the other person's feelings. Please stick to your decision if you feel that's right. The emotional outburst of the opposite party shouldn't change your decision, as that will cause more harm than good.

If you are not the one wanting out of the relationship, then you might be in for a shock. In spite of this, if you can exercise a little self-control, then it will be good for your mental well-being. Getting helpless and saying 'let's try this one more time' or 'I cannot live without you' or making threats like 'you see what I'm going to do now' or cursing 'you will never be happy' is of no use. If you don't know how to react, it's better to remain quiet. After a few days, once the first emotional tide subsides, you can express your point of view in a better and calmer manner.

After the break-up, some days are bound to be bad, and you may face difficulty in functioning for a few days.

Being in love is an addiction. At least our brain interprets it that way, as the dynamics of addiction work here as well. People initially drink alcohol once in a while to cope with the heartbreak, then it becomes a habit. You might also face withdrawal symptoms such as restlessness and anxiety. When you get emotionally attached to a person, you end up talking and meeting almost every day. So, it is only natural that after the separation, you feel restless and anxious and even depressed. But the good part is that just as quicky as this 'withdrawal effect' sets in, it subsides in a few days' time too. But we need to give it time. Therefore, expecting to become normal immediately is wrong. We must accept repeated unwanted, irritating thoughts for a few days and we should also learn to react less to these thoughts so that our days are less troubled.

We may have a whole plethora of emotions for the person

with whom the break-up has happened. We may feel anger and hatred at one point and affection at others. We may feel like going back to that person. But these extremes of emotions and thoughts are temporary. 'Should I go back?' or 'let me call once' are our weak moments, and you should not give in. To handle these weak moments, keep small slips of paper with you. Write down why the relationship didn't work and how much you suffered as a result. Carry these slips in your wallet. Fond memories may be triggered by looking at anything, such as a coffee shop or even a bus stop or old photographs. To control these emotions, carry these slips of paper with you at all times. Repeatedly tell yourself: what's the solution to gangrene? Amputation is the only way, and what has happened has happened for the best.

Many patients ask if they can remain friends with their ex. Well, the truth is: some people can manage that, some cannot. It's better not to have any communication for at least six months to a year when the wound is still raw and just the sight of the person might lead to the upheaval of confusing thoughts and conflicting feelings. If you are able to see each other as just friends after that period, then you can continue communicating. If you remain in touch immediately after the break-up, then thoughts like 'Why is she calling me every day?' or 'Seems like I am still special for him, he is still sharing everything with me' may arise. These are torture for the mind. You might also think 'I am feeling so much pain and he appears so happy when I talk to him', which is also difficult to digest. Respect yourself and don't keep any contact. If you work in the same office or share the same friend circle, then maintain only basic formal communication.

Now a little bit on how to spend these difficult days.

Whenever we face trying times in life, a one-day-at-a-time

approach is very useful. Plan for the day and don't think much about the future, because thinking about the future in this period only causes anxiety. Write down your priorities for this period and start working on them. Make a list of the things that make you happy and do at least three such things in a day. Try to focus on other meaningful and important relationships. You may have been ignoring them when you were in a romantic relationship. Strengthen your relationship with your parents and friends.

Don't discuss what went wrong in this relationship with too many people. It is human nature to be partial when we discuss our story, hiding our own mistakes. So, discussing it serves no purpose except to entertain people.

The majority of break-ups don't happen in the right manner, and both parties end up insulting each other. As a result, your confidence may take a hit and you may even feel an inferiority complex. If somebody rejects us, or breaks up with us doesn't mean that we are inferior to anybody. Many circumstantial factors are involved in such cases. But do try to note what you learned from this failed relationship.

Try to set small achievable goals and start working towards them to build your confidence.

One important note: if you are unable to come out of this stressful situation even after some time has passed and you are still feeling depressed, then please consult a psychiatrist. These are general guidelines, but in individual consultations, counselling is customized to the individual's needs. Some of the medicines that we use to treat depression are very useful in patients who have recently had a break-up. They reduce the preoccupation with repetitive thoughts, rejection sensitivity and a constant desire to call/meet that person or check their social media profile.

Having a break-up is very common in the beautiful formative

years of our life, but it should not act as a disruption; rather, it should be a stepping stone, enriching our emotional world and experiences.

Marital discord

Tensions and stressors have always existed in married life, but the instances of separation and divorce have increased greatly in the last few years.

Currents of self-awareness and independence have become very strong in the last few years. Men and women are both well-educated nowadays, and both parties are financially independent as well. The average marriage age has also increased. As per psychology, our flexibility to adjust to new situations reduces as we age. Therefore, while we may think of settling down after being stable financially and professionally, it can sometimes become a roadblock to our personal growth. This doesn't mean you should get married early or that you should get married before being settled. We need to accept these changes in how people live, and they are good as well. But this can't be at the cost of family, which is getting less importance nowadays.

Family is often the principal motivation for the struggles we take up. No matter what we face in our life—insults, humiliation—the family is the place where we feel valued and respected and where we find support. That's why we should try to save our marriage and family as far as possible through marital counselling or couple therapy. Marital counselling is not only suggested for couples who are on the verge of a divorce but also for couples who have ongoing frictions that may act as triggers for mental illnesses if not properly addressed.

There may be various reasons behind every divorce and

separation, but this framework of counselling can be helpful in the initial sittings.

A person requires an average of 6–12 months to accept and adapt to the changes that happen after marriage, irrespective of whether it is a love marriage or an arranged marriage. The natural tendency initially is to resist the changes, good or bad. It takes time to understand the difference between your 'ideal partner' and your 'real partner'. The first step is to get used to the presence of your spouse, followed by development of 'feelings' for them. During this initial period of marriage, it's advised to be patient and not make any hurried decisions.

After this initial period passes, any disagreements are best handled by a close friend or unbiased family member who wants the best for both. If disagreements persist, it's best to visit a psychiatrist as a second step.

Even though every divorce might have varied reasons behind it, marital counselling can be of immense help in most cases. In the first sitting of marital counselling, the psychiatrist analyses if either of the partners has developed mental illness due to marital stress or any other reasons. It could well be that the issues in the marriage are because of an existing mental illness. Proper treatment of the illness in that case can reduce the need for marital counselling.

Then comes the most important part of counselling—identifying the habits and behaviours that the partners cannot stand in each other. Your partner should be aware of the things you will never compromise on. People have varied limits of acceptability. For example, one might not tolerate their husband's drinking habit, while another may be okay with it but not the abuses in their state of inebriation. That is the reason why the spouse/partner must be aware of the list of things that will never be compromised on.

We ask both partners to make a list of these points. Here, we have to work with both of them to find a mutually agreeable solution.

Apart from this list, a list of other things that each one has been compromising on so far and is okay doing in the future too is equally important. Often, the spouse is not aware of the compromises their partner has been making in the past.

The counsellor also asks them about the good qualities of their spouse and any good memories they have of them. Keeping such things in writing and referring those at moments of anger can help clients calm down immediately.

'Why am I still in this marriage?' This is the most important question that must be answered very clearly by both the spouses. The reasons could be many: shared responsibilities such as children and ageing parents, the fear of being alone, societal pressure, financial dependency and so on. But the conclusion is the same—they want to remain in the marriage. Recollecting these reasons during stressful periods helps a person calm down.

During marital counselling, we ask clients to avoid verbal fights with the spouse, as it is destructive and brings up unnecessary incidents from the past. Instead, written communication, say, via emails and messages, should be preferred. If really required, it's advised to condemn the behaviour of the spouse, not the person. Instead of saying 'You are a bad person, you always make this mistake' say, 'You should not have reacted to my comment in such a manner'. It always pays to be specific.

Most importantly, both partners are taught to praise each other for small things done for them by their partner. With time, people typically forget to praise their spouse and start taking things for granted.

For most women, their in-laws is a sensitive topic. Marital counselling can change the behaviour of the spouse but not of the in-laws. It is difficult for a person to change at old age. We all have some discomforts, minor ailments and complaints about our own body. Do we ever feel like discarding this body and wish to have someone else's body? No, we don't. The way we accept our body with its existing issues, we need to accept our in-laws as our own.

We suggest you talk to your spouse at least half an hour every day on any topic and encourage conversation. In the beginning, most couples have to make an extra effort and may feel that it's unnatural, but it helps reduce relationship stress in the long run.

Make a list of what your spouse likes and make an effort to take interest in those activities.

Try to sincerely follow the above-mentioned tips for at least six months. Initially these may feel mechanical, but it becomes easier and more natural with time. The French biographer, novelist and essayist André Maurois has put it so aptly: 'A successful marriage is an edifice that must be built every day'.[28]

Infidelity

This is a very sensitive topic in marriage and often one of the primary reasons why couples seek marital therapy. However, it's often a result of a dysfunctional marriage rather than the cause.

Long-standing dissatisfaction with the existing relationship—particularly involving boredom, lack of communication, a perception that the marriage is a bond without respect, full of criticism and a chronically poor physical relationship, and

---

[28] Anderson, Chandrama, 'Couples: "A successful marriage is an edifice that must be rebuilt every day"', *Palo Alto Online*, 8 June 2018, https://bit.ly/3MUZC2z. Accessed on 17 March 2022.

difficulty in controlling socially and morally unacceptable urges and opportunities outside of the marriage to seek emotional or physical pleasure—is often a cocktail common in infidelity cases. I have also seen many times in my clinical practice that when there are certain stressful circumstances in the marriage, such as a disabled child or an elderly parent who needs constant care and supervision, infidelity serves as an escape and a distraction to get some pleasure in an otherwise dull and stressful life.

The question that arises then is: how to handle the partner's betrayal in the marriage?

In a live-in relationship, the couple can separate, but in marriage, it's a difficult call to take, as there is usually collective involvement in several spheres—financial, emotional, social and legal. There is often a great deal of interdependence in day-to-day life and in raising children. And when it comes to infidelity, how much is too much is a million-dollar question. Research involving 90,000 men and women found that 78.6 per cent of men and 91.6 per cent of women admitted to having engaged in emotional infidelity.[29] And this has gone up with easy access to social media. While the exact statistics of emotional infidelity are not known, its prevalence is higher than physical infidelity. When it comes to physical infidelity, 20–25 per cent of men commit it and 10–13 per cent of the women commit it.[30]

---

[29] Vinopal, Lauren, 'More People Are Having Emotional Affairs Than Are Not', *Fatherly*, 5 September 2018, https://bit.ly/38a2kSb. Accessed on 17 March 2022.

[30] Zuckerman, Arthur, '50 Cheating Statistics: 2020/2021 Demographics, Reasons & Who Cheats More', *CompareCamp*, 29 May 2020, https://bit.ly/3COoF2q. Accessed on 17 March 2022; Russell, Tonya ,'New Findings Show Divide in How Men and Women View Infidelity', *VerywellMind*, 7 September 2020, https://bit.ly/3Ii59fW. Accessed on 17 March 2022.

Women tend to react more strongly to emotional infidelity committed by their husband. It's very difficult for the woman to digest that her husband was emotionally involved with some other woman 24/7 as opposed to having a physical encounter lasting a few minutes. However, both kinds of infidelity are very hurtful.

When it comes to men, they find physical infidelity more devastating than their spouse's emotional involvement with other men.

Regardless of what kind of infidelity is taking place in a marriage, it's devastating and needs major work and help for both parties to find coping mechanisms, either together or separately. We need to give time for the spouses to figure out their exact emotions, what they want to say or hear from each other and what call they want to take. Many of them need calming medications for controlling anger and feelings of hurt and anxiety. Some even require medications to help them sleep better.

In the initial stages, the chances of domestic violence are high, and we ask them to practise better ways of anger channelization. As time passes, they understand the trauma they are experiencing and decide in a balanced state of mind what to do about it. Normally, there are three options:

i. They are unable to accept the act of infidelity and decide to separate.
ii. They decide to live together happily and also make attempts to rebuild the relationship. They also make serious attempts to try to put behind them what had happened.
iii. They stay together, harass their spouse regarding the infidelity and make life hell for each other.

The third option is the worst and cannot serve any positive purpose in the long run to either of the partners. Hence, it must be avoided.

If the partners decide to stay together even after the occurrence of infidelity, the process of marital therapy begins with the partners, along with therapy for overcoming the trauma of being cheated on. Steps are also taken to manage the emotions and needs of both partners.

Infidelity can break a marriage or act as an opportunity for reshaping it.

Death

I am yet unsure of the concept of rebirth, but I do know that people are reborn with the death of every loved one.

When a loved one dies, they take a part of us with them. This occurrence has the power to turn to dust all our plans for life, all our ambitions and desires. It can severely shake our belief system and we may lose faith in ourselves, in other relationships and in God as well. The fundamentals of our life are affected. After an indefinite time, this whirlwind stops. We start organizing our life again, we start accepting the absence of the departed person at a formal, informal and personal level, we start learning to take up some of their responsibilities and we again learn how to live without that person.

These are inevitable events that happen in everyone's life at some or the other time. Although we never wish to, we are left with no choice but to face them to the best of our abilities and resources, and most of us manage to come out of the grief after a variable time. Then what's the purpose of this topic? Although the majority of people come out of grief in three to six months' time, there are some who carry the burden of non-healing, ulcerating wounds like Ashwatthama[31] for years and years. How to avoid that and how to deal with this irreversible event are very important, and that's what I would like to address below.

When a dear one dies, the people around them go through different stages of grief. All these stages are influenced by factors such as premature and untimely death or the person's position in the family. What were their responsibilities? In what circumstances did the death happen?

The first stage of grief is denial and shock. We receive the news, but our mind may not be able to accept it. There could be disbelief or a feeling of numbness. Often people behave strangely or may not even feel the exact emotions. This emotionally numb stage is actually good for finishing the mechanical tasks and formalities like arranging the funeral, informing the relatives, getting important paperwork done, etc.

Gradually, with the visits of relatives and friends at home and repeated discussions and revisions of how and what happened, all levels of our mind accept the actual loss we are facing, and here starts the phase of anger and frustration—the second phase of coming out of grief. Anger could be directed at the doctors, at life, at God, at relatives and friends too. If the death has happened in unnatural circumstances such as an accident or murder, then anger increases greatly.

---

[31] During his birth, along with immortality, Ashwatthama was awarded a glittering gemstone in the centre of his forehead. He fought the Pandavas on the Kaurava's side. When in a fit of rage, he aimed his Brahmastra at Abhimanyu's fetus growing in Uttara's womb. Krishna was infuriated and took away the stone from his forehead as a punishment, cursing him to bear the pain of this non-healing wound forever. Similarly, many people who experience the trauma of grief beyond a time limit carry that wound in the mind for long periods.

The third stage of grief is characterized by the 'if and buts' phase, that is, the phase of bargaining. Here, we think of questions such as 'If I had come to know about this earlier...' or 'If I hadn't allowed him to go out that day...' or 'If only I hadn't admitted him over there...', etc. Our dreams at the time are also related to the deceased person. For example, we can have dreams related to their illness—we see the deceased person getting better and recovering. This happens because although we have accepted the reality, a relentless desire of the unconscious mind to get that person back in our life is expressed through our dreams. Many a time, in a market or in crowded places, we may think we have seen the deceased person and misidentify them with someone else.

In the next stage, we understand we have to spend the rest of our life without that person and we often feel helpless over the situation or feel depressed. For some time, we may show all features of depression too. If suffering from depression, we may hold ourselves responsible for whatever has happened and may feel inappropriately guilty.

The last stage is acceptance, where we understand this was destined to happen in the manner it did. The earlier doubts and questions we had in our mind begin to recede and we realize that we can live our life without this person, with a big bunch of bittersweet memories.

One thing we should understand is that although most people go through all these stages, some may directly reach the stage of acceptance immediately after the incident. Second, some may never reach the stage of acceptance. Many people live in the phase of depression. There is no fixed measure of how much time it will take to traverse each phase, but most people come to terms with the reality within six months and resume their normal routine within two years. Also, it is worth mentioning that some people oscillate between the stage of anger and depression and the stage of acceptance for some time. In many emotional ups and downs of life, memories may become stronger and we may go back to the previous stages, but most of the time, these reactions are temporary and we again quickly reach the phase of acceptance.

Here are a few tips that could be useful for most of us when dealing with this situation.

- We should understand that we will face emotional ups and downs for many days. We may feel relaxed and light sometimes and an overwhelming burden at others. There is nothing unnatural about this. If we acknowledge it, the distress reduces.
- 'Enough is enough now, start working' or 'You got normal so quickly'—such statements are mostly made by near and dear ones out of empathy. Many people don't know what to say at such times. Sometimes they may say, 'Is your mourning going to bring him back?' or 'You are old enough, you should know how to control this'. This may not be something we want to hear or may not sound appropriate to us, but we should look at the intention behind their words, which is that we must become normal soon. And we should focus on the intention. If someone is pushing you towards normalcy, don't resume your routine in a hurry just for their sake; do it slowly, allowing your mind to accept the responsibilities. It's better to inform your workplace about the incident. We may not expect any concessions at work, but sometimes we may need a break.
- When such a life-changing incident happens, we should not think about long-term plans. Thinking long term increases our restlessness and worries. We should work on one day at

a time. Second, doing simple day-to-day routine activities regularly helps keep the mind calm during this period.
- Open your heart to your close ones. You may express your worries, pain, stress and helplessness and also talk about the jealousy you feel when you see others happy, if that's how you feel. Talk about your feeling of guilt and anger over the line of treatment given in the hospital, etc. As time passes, we mostly accept that this was destined to happen. I remember a quote of the American author Neale Donald Walsch which is relevant in this context—'Nothing in this universe occurs by accident'.[32]
- Writing a letter to the deceased is also one very effective means of catharsis.
- Everyone grieves in a different manner. If near and dear ones start working normally, one should not conclude they are out of pain.
- Only we can decide what we should feel. Don't think what people will think, say, if you wear good clothes or if you treat yourself to an ice cream. People have their own issues to handle and they don't think much about us. Second, people talk from both sides.
- We are going to follow the same path as our deceased relative sooner or later. Nobody is here permanently. This simple realization is also enough to start living again for good, right?
- We feel better by talking to people who have, like us, grieved in the past. We can get guidance on how they handled the situation, how they got better, etc.
- Spiritual gurus definitely help us, although everyone's path of spirituality may differ. Our science stops at diseases and

---

[32] Walsh, Neale Donald, *Quotes, Goodreads*, https://bit.ly/37wCgQt. Accessed on 17 March 2022.

their possible treatment. Spirituality begins where science ends. Where you cannot reach by science you can reach by faith. Many *jeevas* (souls) are dying every day, many are taking birth. This cycle has been continuing infinitely. Hence, it is a big proof that we are united at the source.
- Some people may experience complicated grief, the symptoms of which are remaining mournful for long period of time, seeing the deceased person or hearing their voice, and not being able to work. A psychiatrist's help is needed at this stage and medicines and therapy are definitely helpful.

When we think about the mortal frame of the body, there are limitations to togetherness. But death has taken only the body of that person. After death, our relationship is intact with the deceased, our memories are intact, signs of their existence are intact, our love and affection remain intact. Is this not a limitation of death?

Exam stress

Examination is the life-long companion of every student. In reality, exams help us finish our syllabus and studies in time, give good momentum to our life and are one of the very important catalysts for the completion of our goals. So, they are actually our friend!

Examinations, whether in the academic domain or in other walks of life, actually help us break our own limitations and understand our true potential. Despite this positive aspect of exams, many of the students suffer from depression, anxiety and stress before and/or after exams. Many psychiatric illnesses may originate during this period. The below-mentioned points could be useful to minimize exam stress.

Although ideally, we need to prepare for exams throughout the year, the last few months are of paramount importance. The most important way to address exam stress is to prepare properly, starting at least three months before the exams. Over the period leading up to the exams, adopt habits that help you study better, such as gathering all the required material first, choosing a well-lit place for studies, preparing a proper schedule/time-table, taking sufficient breaks, and having a proper diet and adequate sleep. Revise what you are studying on a daily basis and have discussions with your friends as well. Mental preparation is equally important. Stay away from distractions and also friends and relatives who lower your morale or put you down. Develop a positive and healthy mindset. Instead of thinking, 'I don't want to study but I have to', look at exams as a means to achieve your goals.

Many a time, due to excessive stress, you may feel restless or have butterflies in the stomach. You may not get adequate restorative sleep. Deep breathing and light exercise are useful at such times. Herbal pills such as ashwagandha can also help. Ask yourself: what exactly is scaring me about this examination? How are the results going to affect me? Write down the answers to these questions.

To block negative thoughts, use thought-stopping methods. For example, wear a rubber band around your wrist throughout the day. Whenever you feel your mind is wandering towards unnecessary or unpleasant things, snap the rubber band. The pain stimulus on the wrist dissociates our mind from that thought. Another thought-stopping method is to imagine a policeman with a rod in his hand hitting you on the back whenever you think about unnecessary thoughts. If you feel the stress is overwhelming, please consult a psychiatrist. We have excellent medicines for stress and anxiety that can be used effectively. They don't have side effects, such as excessive sleep or weight gain, as is commonly believed.

At the time of the exam, adopting some simple strategies can help you do your best and ensure that you don't perform poorly due to stress. For example, reaching the venue early can give you some time to adjust to the setting.

Avoid discussing with friends just before the exam starts. If by chance you are unable to recall something during those conversations, your confidence goes down and it can adversely affect your performance. Read something quietly or engage in deep breathing to keep yourself calm and focussed.

Sometimes, we might go blank or lose the flow of thought while solving the paper. It is very natural and happens to the best of us, so do not panic. Instead, leave that question for a while. Address the next question and come back to this when you feel relaxed. Keep yourself well hydrated by drinking sips of water every now and then, as it keeps the brain refreshed and prevents drowsiness.

Review your answer sheet after the exam, but don't get trapped in that. We are going to take many examinations in our life. Whatever the result, at least your studies won't be in vain, especially your degree examinations. This is because academics are important for our career. A delay of six months or a year here and there doesn't change the equation of life.

Second, an examination evaluates us only academically. Personal and circumstantial angles are not evaluated, even when they affect our performance. If we want to grow as a human being, then the result of academic examination is just one factor; we need to grow and mature on the personal, social and moral levels as well, and there is no formal examination for these.

Not only does the prevalence of stress and mental illnesses increase during exam periods, suicides and suicide attempts do too. If there is an infection in the body, then do we take medicines to get rid of it or do we take poison to kill ourselves? In our future that is replete with infinite possibilities, a failure in an academic examination is a very minuscule thing.

So, instead of considering an exam as a question of life and death, if we consider it as an annual opportunity to help us achieve our dreams and goals faster, then stress will turn into excitement. The difference is only in our thinking.

Parenting

There is a wonderful saying by Oscar Wilde: 'Children begin by loving their parents. After a time they judge them. Rarely, if ever, do they forgive them.'[33] Almost all of us love and respect our parents, most of us feel some anger about their past behaviour or about decisions they made which according to us were not entirely correct.

Here are some challenges faced by parents in an urban setting that make them more prone to stress and subsequently depression:

- **Lack of a support system**: Most families are nuclear in cities. Grandparents often visit their children and support them in rearing their grandchildren, but most of them resist the idea of shifting permanently, as they find it difficult to adjust to the city life. Although there are crèches and day-care centres for working parents, most of them find it difficult to avail these facilities during the initial few months. Taking leaves and running the show when either of the partners or the child is unwell or when either of

---

[33]Wilde, Oscar, *The Picture of Dorian Gray*, Fingerprint! Publishing, 2015.

the partners is travelling is quite difficult for most couples.
- **Extended working hours**: Most of the corporate-sector employees spend a minimum of eight to 10 hours at the workplace on working days and may be a couple of hours in commuting. This reduces leisure time, so most weekends are spent lazily in bed, and a lack of productivity and dullness often supervenes on weekends.
- **Less time spent with children and compensation given through material things**: As most of the time is spent at work, both parents try to compensate by giving all the material things their child asks for. It's a way to get rid of the guilt of not spending enough time with the children. The child doesn't learn to hear 'no' for most things and gets whatever they demand, which, in turn, makes them stubborn and impatient. They often find it difficult to digest rejections in life where the parents are powerless, such as not getting admission in a specific college or when their love interest rejects them, which makes them prone to breakdown and subsequent depression.
- **Gadget addiction**: Although this is an issue faced by people of all age groups, it is a lot more common in children and teens. Due to boredom, fewer real-life experiences and easy access to gadgets, children get addicted to their phones and laptops. Many have unsupervised access to these gadgets for hours. This affects their sleep and productivity. It increases the anger and aggression in them. If the parents are not at home due to work commitments, the addiction worsens.
- **Excessive expectations from kids**: As parents provide all material amenities to their children—expensive schooling, private coaching and curated hobby classes—there is a great deal of expectation from the children to excel in these domains. When these expectations are not met, it becomes

a matter of stress for the family.
- **Financial crunches for the child's education**: I know many people who cannot consider having two kids due to the heavy financial burden of maintaining a family of four and especially sponsoring the children's education.

Parenting is responsible for the mental well-being of a child. Many adult patients we see in the psychiatry OPD are struggling with their childhood issues such as an inferiority complex and wrong self-destructive beliefs knowingly or unknowingly imposed by their parents. To minimize the mistakes of parenting, to understand our child better and to enjoy the whole process is the objective of these pointers.

Let's first understand the different types of parenting and how they influence your child:

- **Strict and over-vigilant parenting**: These parents are very demanding. They usually inflict tough punishment on the child. They do not want the child to take independent decisions. Such a tense environment negatively influences the child. The child lacks confidence, curiosity and decision-making skills.
- **Pessimistic parenting**: These parents do not guide and shape the child. They maintain some distance from the child. They always try to find reasons to not spend time with the child and try to make up for it by providing them with material comforts. While growing up in such a depressing environment, the child feels neglected.
- **Friendly and disciplined parenting**: These parents decide the rules and limitations by being inclusive with the child and taking them into confidence in a friendly manner. The children have freedom and their rights are respected. Expectations are set such that they are not a burden on the

child. Children growing in such an environment become responsible, independent, confident and good citizens.

Friendly and disciplined parenting is considered the best. The following pointers can be useful in implementing this style of parenting. These pointers are especially applicable for children aged one to 10 years, as parenting for teenagers is slightly different.

- The parents' expectations should match the child's age.
- Don't criticize the child, criticize their behaviour—there is a difference. If you need to make comparisons at all, compare them with their past performances. Give them the confidence and motivation to face challenges and failures.
- Inculcate discipline in the child in a friendly manner and discuss beforehand the consequences of breaking rules.
- Learn to say 'no' to the child's unreasonable demands. Give them the reasoning behind your refusal in the most easy and understandable way.
- Time out is a better form of punishment than punishing them physically. Always give the reason behind the punishment and don't let the child go to bed without closure to the event.
- Children learn by watching their parents—be a role model for them and behave/act in the way you want your child to. If you want the child to reduce gadget time, ideally you should too. Walk the talk.
- Ask the child to share what happened in school, and listen without interruptions.
- Discuss with them the important events happening in the country, society and in your vicinity. Seek their opinion. Tell them though your viewpoints may differ, you are united at heart.

- Focus beyond academics—on exercise, playtime, giving children some responsibility, developing skills, etc.
- Saying 'I love you' is not enough. Show that you mean those three words.
- Both the parents should have a single opinion about important events, especially in front of the child. They should be united in their decisions; otherwise it will confuse the child.

At the end, parents are almost godly for the child. If parents are more aware, then projection of these virtues can be more effective and the outcomes will also be better.

Elderly care

Some of the common complaints youngsters have against their elderly parents (typically senior citizens) are: 'Mother has changed, she is not the same as the one who raised me', 'She gets angry quickly, she is very stubborn', 'Father has become very slow these days; he takes a lot of time in the bathroom and for his meals, and he has become very forgetful', 'Mother-in-law cannot hear properly, then how come she can hear what I am saying to my mother in a low voice?', 'Father doesn't remember daily errands related to marketing, but remembers all the older incidences'. We can get answers to all these questions if we attempt to understand what old age is. As we grow old, our body as well as our mind undergo changes, even if we don't realize it. We will now try to understand the connection between these changes and the questions raised above and what could be the potential solutions. We will also try to understand how to take care of the elderly at home.

Everyone goes through what we call *utpatti*, *sthiti* and

laya. During childhood, our body and mind grow; this is the utpatti stage. In adulthood, we reach the status of sthiti, and during old age, our body and mind slow down. As we age (laya), immunity reduces, we are more prone to infections, and we potentially develop arthritis, weaker bones and long-sightedness. The basic senses—hearing, touch and taste become weak. Our heart size increases, blood pressure fluctuates, heartbeat becomes irregular, digestion weakens and supply of blood to the brain decreases.

Changes happening in the mind are more evident to others. The elderly person is generally not aware of them. They tend to forget recent events, even though older memories are not easily lost. The speed of working and thinking reduces. Multitasking becomes difficult—'Keep an eye on your grandchild as well as the gas stove'—this is almost impossible for them to do. They get confused and irritated easily. The front part of the brain responsible for control over selfish feelings gets depleted, and stubbornness and selfishness increase.

Just like younger people, the elderly too have to tackle many questions and tests, such as keeping oneself healthy, how to avoid becoming dependent on others. They have to be prepared to handle the reduction in their capacity to work and various organs slowly giving away. They spend their time revisiting the past, trying not to get disturbed by it.

Often their spouse or friends are no longer with them and they need to live with that. They will have to find ways to keep themselves occupied during these years. Their relationship with children and grandchildren is going to change with time, so they need to accept that.

Apart from this, with time, their responsibilities change and while fulfilling them, they realize their new limitations. In some cases, they have no support from the family.

There are a few ways in which a family member can recognize the needs of the elderly and take adequate care of them. Don't think 'Oh, I know what they like and dislike'. With time and age, the likes and dislikes change, and it's best to ask and not assume anything. If you receive unexpected replies for questions such as what changes they expect in their lifestyle or if the family or caretaker is lacking somewhere, do not react immediately, but think about what they have said. If you closely observe their behaviour, you can make out their mental state. For example, eating less than usual or sitting alone indicates that something is amiss. If we are unable to understand them or their mental state, it's important to consult a psychiatrist.

A few common needs of the elderly are listed below; not everything is applicable to all.

- **Need for security**: This need increases with age as vision and hearing reduce in the elderly and they become susceptible to a fall. A well-lit room makes them feel secure. Also, install handles and supports in bathrooms and stairs. Important telephone numbers written down in large font and an alarm bell can also be provided.
- **Need for freedom and independence**: It's important to preserve their freedom and self-reliance till the very end. For example, let them go out on their own but make sure they have their identity card, address and brief information about their diseases with them. Their day-to-day activities should be linked with some important activities, such as taking their medication post lunch. It's important to check the remaining medication from time to time to ensure it is being taken properly. Observing them from time to time when they are out, obviously without them knowing about it, can help ensure they don't get lost. Financial independence is

also very important. Giving them a fixed amount of money to spend every month is a good practice. That will restore confidence in their analytical skills as well.

- **Need for communication**: When you are young, you are surrounded by people, but you don't have time to talk to them. The elderly have a lot of time at their disposal but unfortunately, very few people to give them company. The solution to this problem is to make time for them, listen more and talk less. Also, you can take out old photographs and discuss the memories associated with them.
- **Need for complete acceptance**: Don't apply older references or contexts. Now the elderly have changed and so have the contexts. Limit your expectations. As they grow old, a person may not be able to provide emotional support to the family members. We need to accept them with their illnesses and limitations.
- **Need for love and compassion**: Simple gestures like massaging their legs, cleaning their room, combing their hair, etc. are good ways to show your love, and doing such things from time to time helps them feel loved and accepted. Old people should be involved in discussions around critical and important issues at home.
- **Need for self-confidence and creation**: Set small goals for the elderly and help them nurture hobbies they could not pursue before. Give them some responsibilities. Split them into small goals and once achieved, praise them. If they don't know how to use a computer or a smartphone, teach them. Help them mingle with people their age—this will fulfil their social needs and build self-confidence.

The elderly face many difficulties such as increasing stubbornness, anger, irritability, forgetfulness, mental disturbance, fear and suspicion, and lack of sleep. While handling these, remember that we don't have solutions that will be applicable to all. Second, even if they do raise their voice at us, we may not be the target—the real reason may be something totally different, such as constipation or a simple change of environment. Irritability may also increase because they aren't able to express what they want or understand what the family member/helper is trying to say.

To avoid all these issues, try to identify the cause. Fixing a routine for the elderly that includes exercise and music helps. Ask them to solve crossword puzzles or sudoku to improve memory. All these issues have good remedy in psychiatry, and one can always benefit from them.

Job loss

This is a major cause of stress in urban life. Many of us choose to live in big cities for the sake of work. Deflation in some sectors every year causes a lot of job insecurity, and many companies choose to downsize. Job loss doesn't just affect us financially; it also takes a toll on the mind. Many people feel that their self-esteem is compromised. They start viewing their life as purposeless. They miss the social connectedness the job offered. Although getting a job is only partially in our control, by the time we can find another one, these simple methods can boost the affected person's morale and bring out a stronger version of them. These methods can be called 'GO BACK TO JOB':

- **G**: Get adequate rest, sleep well, exercise and eat healthy. Feelings of unrest and losing sleep over factors beyond your control will only make things worse.

- **O**: Occupy your mind in some creative pursuit. We all know that an idle mind is a devil's workshop. Channel out in some long due activity or skill you wanted to learn.
- **B**: Read biographies. Reading books and watching movies based on the real-life challenges of someone inspirational can motivate us, besides having entertainment value. When we learn about how others fought their way out of struggles and tough times, it restores hope.
- **A**: Accept the reality. Accepting and acknowledging the reality is crucial, as it stops you from dwelling in the past and going through a needless blame game with the self and with others involved.
- **C**: Connect with dear ones and yourself too. Utilize this time to connect with family and to strengthen this unit. Also, connect with yourself and reflect on your life and goals.
- **K**: Brush up your knowledge. Getting a job is only partially in our control, but sharpening our knowledge and updating ourselves is entirely in our hands.
- **T**: Talk to a psychiatrist if you are showing signs of depression for over two weeks. Talking to a psychiatrist on time can prevent further emotional issues.
- **O**: Stay off negative people—negative friends and relatives who have a problem with everything you do. Such people often bring down our morale. Cut them off for the time being.
- **J**: Journaling about your achievements and the things you are grateful for is a great way to boost self-esteem. Write about academic and non-academic achievements too. Also, write down the things you are grateful for, as it changes your perspective to life.
- **O**: Opportunities can be found in the same and parallel areas. See if a minor or major role change is required as per the demands in your discipline and implement it.

- **B**: Boost your self-esteem through positive self-dialogues and affirmations. The most important thing to say is 'This job loss doesn't define me, it's a setback, but I have more resources, more strength to bounce back.'

Infertility problems

Conception literally happens in the womb, but in infertility patients, the conception of a baby happens in the mind before happening in the womb at the very start of treatment! As stated correctly—*already in my heart, someday in my arms*. People carry thoughts of the yet-to-be conceived baby right from when they begin the infertility treatment. Hence, taking care of their mind through this journey is of paramount value.

As per statistics from the Indian Society for Assisted Reproduction (ISAR), the issue of infertility is seen in almost 10–14 per cent of the Indian population. The urban population is affected even more, and one in every six couples trying to conceive suffers from infertility. Nearly 27.5 million couples actively trying to conceive suffer from infertility in India.[34]

For the majority of couples diagnosed with infertility, stress plays a vicious role. Stress intensifies the factors causing infertility, and infertility in turn increases stress.

For many patients, life comes to a standstill till conception. They report social awkwardness and their life is often stuck in following important dates with respect to the monthly cycle. Many people cannot go outside for holidays and have to postpone their travel plans. Planning for the future also comes to a halt.

Time away from work could induce stress, as many are not

---

[34]Lal, Neeta, 'India's Hidden Infertility Struggles', *The Diplomat*, 30 May 2018, https://bit.ly/3N9TV0X. Accessed on 17 March 2022.

comfortable sharing the real reason for their absences/leaves.

The treatments are often lengthy and exhausting in all ways, with no promised outcome, and each failed cycle adds to despair for the couple. Even before the actual periods (menstrual flow) begins, with the onset of premenstrual symptoms like skin breakouts, oily skin, bloating, etc., the majority of women sense the impending periods and go through the phase of lows, irritability and difficulty coping with the fact that this cycle's attempt too was a failure. This phase usually lasts for a week to 10 days. Interpersonal difficulties may arise in some couples, including issues with respect to intimacy. Many couples who come for fertility treatment report their lifestyles had been quite busy, as is typical in urban life, and that they had very little time for communication and intimacy. Sexual dysfunction can be a cause of infertility, but often it's the result of infertility. Another frequent observation is that marriage at an advanced age can also be a problem for conception, particularly for women, where fertility rapidly declines after a certain age. After a late marriage, many couples want to plan a family only after getting to know each other better, which is a right thought in its own way but can be challenging for conception.

Social and family pressure is significant in Indian culture. Having a child is a matter of pride and social status for many families, so pressure builds up every month after a few years of marriage.

Couples undergoing infertility treatment often choose a self-imposed isolation to avoid nagging questions from relatives and friends in their social circle. They avoid mixing with people who have kids, as it evokes mixed feelings. Many couples in fact skip weddings and other social functions in their home town to avoid the salvo of questions. I remember one of my patients reported that when she shifted to a new apartment, the neighbours asked her which school she was considering for her kids. Instead of asking a more general question like 'Who all are there in your family?', people end up asking 'How many kids do you have?'.

One has to be financially strong for advanced fertility treatments like IVF. Many couples have family responsibilities or loans to pay, and most insurance companies don't cover the cost of fertility treatments. This takes a toll as well.

Third-party conception and single parenting are further big issues. When people consider having a child from donor eggs or donor sperm, it is not easy to reach a decision. Everyone grieves for the loss of genetic link and many unaddressed and unexpressed emotions and thoughts could build up in both partners' minds. The burden of the choices and their outcomes are quite taxing in such situations.

Pregnancy decisions by the LGBT (lesbian, gay, bisexual and transgender) population and the decision of single parenting require more preparation of the mind than of the body.

And the roller-coaster ride of IVF is another overwhelming event, where the physical pain of the injections is one part and the financial burden is another. Adjustments are required at various levels: in your personal and professional life, during the IVF cycle. Every day brings news before the embryo transfer, i.e. in many circumstances, one has to be ready that a cycle may get cancelled or postponed due to various reasons. The 14-day wait to get the test result is taxing.

It's also difficult to know when to stop seeking treatment. Frequently, one partner wants to end the treatment before the other, which can strain the relationship. Most patients need to gradually, and with great difficulty, make the transition from wanting biological children to accepting that they will have to pursue adoption or come to terms with being childless.

So, infertility affects all aspects of life. Various studies have found that for 50 per cent of women and 15 per cent of men, infertility was the most upsetting experience of their lives.[35] In fact, women with infertility felt as anxious or depressed as those diagnosed with cancer and hypertension or recovering from a heart attack.

What can we do to reduce the stress of this situation?

- Including your partner in everything you are going through often helps. The crux here is communication. Express yourself, listen, cry together and assure and prepare each other for the possible outcomes. The relationship thrives even in this journey of infertility if communication remains intact.
- These are beautiful productive years in most couples' lives, as most of them are between 30 and 45 years of age. Please don't postpone any major plans of your career or your life for something beyond your control. The baby may happen when it has to happen, and that outcome is beyond anyone's control. But do the things that are important to you and are in *your* control.
- Don't allow your intimacy to suffer. The goal of intimacy is not just baby-making. Most couples suffer from intimacy issues with the diagnosis of infertility. Intimacy is helpful for keeping your bond intact and for keeping your stress hormones low.
- Find clever ways to tackle difficult questions asked by people and learn not to take it to heart. When to have a child and whether to have a child is entirely your decision. Many of my patients simply respond

---

[35]Freeman, E.W. et al., 'Psychological evaluation and support in a program of in vitro fertilization and embryo transfer', *Fertility and Sterility*, January 1985; 43(1): 48–53, https://bit.ly/36062Nl. Accessed on 17 March 2022.

with a smile when asked such questions. When your friends or relatives ask questions, you could respond with statements like, 'When that day comes, you will be first to know', or 'Keep your blessings with us'. You can develop your own ways to answer such questions.

- Find time for exercise and yoga, follow a relaxation routine, take your multivitamin supplements regularly and get in shape if you are not. It makes the treatment easier and boosts your self-esteem too.
- Take occasional breaks from the treatment. This acts as a recharge and recuperation break. Go for a vacation and try to avoid discussing the topic during these breaks.
- Join a support group for infertility treatment. There are many who meet in person and there are others that function online.
- Keep a journal. Express your feelings and thoughts regularly in it.
- Talk to a psychiatrist if the situation seems overwhelming. Psychotherapy and medicines have a role in management. Through this, you can develop excellent coping mechanisms and resolve dilemmas and conflicts. Patients feel validated and interpersonal relationships improve. There are also positive biological effects, better performance in terms of intimacy and greater adherence to infertility treatment, which can eventually influence the outcome.

Post-partum blues and depression

Almost 80 per cent of women face post-partum blues, whereas post-partum depression happens to nearly 10 per cent.[36]

---

[36]'Postpartum Psychiatric Disorders', MGH Center for Women's Mental Health, https://bit.ly/3idHwKT. Accessed on 17 March 2022.

As the name indicates, blues are times of tearfulness, confusion, sleeplessness, mood swings and irritability—in other words, overwhelmed feelings due to the new responsibility. They start after delivery and last for the initial couple of weeks after it. The reasons for those are major hormonal changes which happen post-delivery, changes in the body, discomfort and pain, lack of sleep, breastfeeding adjustments, a sudden shift of the relatives' attention and care from the would-be mother in pregnancy to the baby after delivery, and of course, tending to the newborn every two hours. In urban settings, the prevalence of post-partum blues is higher as an extended support system is often lacking, although medical facilities are excellent.

Post-partum depression may start anywhere between four weeks to three months of delivery and is a lot more serious in terms of symptoms with severe depressogenic thoughts. There may even be thoughts of harming yourself and the baby. Post-partum depression needs proper management through medication, but these tips could be helpful:

- Acknowledge your feelings, whatever they may be. Most of the time, people expect a new mother to be on top of the world or bond immediately with the baby. This may not be the case for many first-time mothers. Acknowledge the discomfort or the sense of being overwhelmed and don't feel guilty about it. It gets better gradually.
- Get enough and good sleep. One should sincerely follow grandma's advice: sleep when the baby sleeps. Your body and mind both need it in the post-partum period.
- Make sure you are getting a wholesome and nutritious diet. Often in urban settings, nutrition is ignored due to a lack of helping hands, which causes further anxiety.

A healthy post-partum eating plan is crucial to keep bone loss at bay, replenish your iron reserves, and most importantly, promote milk production. Staying hydrated is very important if you are breastfeeding, as breastmilk is 87 per cent water. So, less water intake can leave you dehydrated and feeling tired. Good protein supplement is generally recommended for the first two months after delivery for quick recovery from post-partum losses. This should be in addition to a good protein-rich diet, which should include legumes, eggs and milk products. Prenatal multivitamin and iron, and calcium supplements should be continued for at least six weeks after delivery. Good munching options include nuts and dry fruits, which are loaded with good fats and antioxidants.

- Connect to new moms over the phone or in a virtual group. Their experiences are very helpful in managing your issues.
- Sleep with the baby and try to establish breastfeeding routine as early as possible. It reduces a lot of stress, promotes bonding and is comforting for you and the baby.
- Set aside some time for yourself. Take a stroll in the sunlight to uplift your mood or sit alone in the balcony with your morning and evening tea/coffee for whatever time you can afford.
- Delegate work at home, learn to say no and don't hesitate to ask for help when you need it.
- Most importantly, everyone takes variable time to get adjusted to this new phase. So, give yourself a reasonable amount of time, say two to four weeks, to develop the bond and wear your new role comfortably.

- If the symptoms worsen over the course of time, please talk to a psychiatrist.

Diagnosis of terminal illness

The diagnosis of a life-limiting illness brings a plethora of emotions and raises multiple issues for patients and their immediate family and close relatives. The issues extend beyond physical suffering and often involve finances, social circle, and various fears like dependency, job loss, relationship changes and death. There may not be scope for a cure, but there is definitely scope for care. From this point of view, to study the effect of the mind on cancers and vice versa, a separate branch called psycho-oncology has been created. Many people are still unaware of the scope of psycho-oncology and the role of the psychiatrist in it.

For each of the issues mentioned earlier, a psychiatrist can help with medicines, which are of great use in uplifting the patient's mood, reducing anxiety and depression, increasing pain tolerance, promoting sleep and improving appetite. A psychiatrist can also offer counselling. Even relatives of the patient need help, particularly if the patient is young.

After all, what we follow in such situations is the age-old saying—a doctor should cure sometimes but comfort always. When asked about their last wishes and the palliative care set-up where I visit, most of the patients wish for a good death—that is, they want the goodbye to happen when they are surrounded by their relatives, preferably in their native and ancestral home, without much trouble to their bodies. In other words, they want to breathe their last among familiar people, in a familiar set-up and without much suffering.

Orientation issues

In a rural set-up, homosexual individuals don't often come out and take up a 'straight lifestyle' due to societal pressure. This proves to be quite suffocating for many, who then move to cities for more freedom. However, life is not easy in an urban set-up either.

The prevalence of homosexuality and bisexuality is almost 3–10 per cent in our community.[37] Although homosexual orientation is as normal as straight orientation as per our science and now the law, too, in India and is not a psychiatric disorder, the prevalence of psychiatric disorders is quite high in this population.[38] There are several reasons for it. The majority of the times, relationships in this community are short lived and come with a lot of insecurity, as there is no societal sanction like marriage. Many have multiple relationships in the early years of their life which impact their psyche substantially. The family and near ones often don't accept this orientation or their partners. Sometimes, in fact, there is a struggle to accept their own orientation, and they may spend many years in confusion and conflicting thoughts. Opposite-sex marriages often happen under family pressure and repetitive questioning by near ones, but the majority of them remain unhappy or dissatisfied in the marriage.

My patients often report that faking happiness and a heterosexual life is a burden on them. For stimulation and for

---

[37] 'Prevalence of Homosexuality, Bisexuality', *CliffsNotes*, https://bit.ly/3KVcGmP. Accessed on 17 March 2022.
[38] Semlyen, Joanna et al., 'Sexual orientation and symptoms of common mental disorder or low wellbeing: combined meta-analysis of 12 UK population health surveys', *BMC Psychiatry*, 67 (2016), https://bit.ly/3KxZUL2. Accessed on 12 April 2022.

reducing inhibitions, many of them consume a variety of drugs and may get addicted to them. As regards men, some of them even get seriously bullied in college and the workplace if their mannerisms are effeminate or their orientation is obvious. Even hate crimes against the LGBTQ community are high. Third-party conceptions by gay and lesbian couples to become parents are also an issue that needs to be addressed. These are the main reasons for depression in this community.

A psychiatrist can help understand the situation better and lead to greater acceptance by the person with alternate orientation and their family members, addressing issues of depression, anxiety and homophobia.

5

I CAN BE MORE RESILIENT

Let's look at two movies before we embark on this topic.

Devdas, a well-made movie based on a novel with the same name, depicts the story of an alcoholic and depressed lover Devdas, who is sober, happy and cheerful in his youth. He is madly in love with his neighbour Paro, and both have a very strong emotional involvement. When they disclose their relationship, both families are opposed against it. Paro unwillingly gets married to a wealthy widower instead. Unable to bear the stress, Devdas adopts poor coping mechanisms to distract himself, gets addicted to alcohol, starts visiting a brothel and befriends a courtesan, who falls in love with him. He suffers from depression and lives in this unhappy state for the rest of his life.

The Pursuit of Happyness is a beautiful movie based on a true story about a man named Christopher Gardner. The hero (Will Smith) faces a big turmoil in his personal and professional life, but he handles everything with patience, maintaining balance and dignity, and channels the energy stemming out of stress in a positive way, finally coming out a winner.

These two examples reiterate how our state of mind governs everything in our life. What can be done to achieve flexibility and resilience in testing times so that we are able to handle such situations in the right manner without losing our mental balance?

What is resilience? What will happen if we try to stretch a piece of glass? It will snap. What if we try to stretch a rubber band? It stretches to a good extent, and if you stretch it further, you will see its elasticity increases. Similarly, by building resilience, we are increasing our adaptability to a variety of stressors, by virtue of which we don't easily fall prey to depression and other psychiatric illnesses.

In this chapter, we will try to understand some basic strategies for managing our stress and negative emotions, and instilling a better lifestyle to keep depression at bay. Does it guarantee that depression will not hit us if we practise this properly? Not really. Both endogenous and exogenous depression can affect us, but the probability definitely reduces. The severity of the depression and anxiety is also less.

Troubled past, unknown future

Most of us dwelling in past or future issues tend to neglect the present.

Two kinds of past really trouble us. The first is where we have been the victim of situations and the second where we were guilty of troubling others. In spite of thinking and replaying these tapes of the past repeatedly in our head, we usually can't find a way out. In fact, by brooding over them, the memories become stronger and darker. They don't serve any positive purpose; instead, they reduce our confidence at critical moments and start torturing us.

Future worries stem from seeing other people's sufferings or negative experiences, and fearing the same could happen to us.

It is possible to avoid this self-torture. The only thing we have to do is make a conscious effort to change the thinking. First, we need to ask ourselves an important question: how long am

I going to carry this heavy baggage of the past? I remember a story relevant to this. Two young monks start travelling towards their gurukul from a village. They have to cross a river to go to the other side. A disabled young lady requests them to help her cross the river. The younger of the two monks immediately takes her on his shoulders and crosses the river. She thanks them and the two monks keep walking towards the gurukul. Two hours later, they arrive at the gurukul. The old monk says to the young monk, 'By holding that young lady, you have committed a grave sin and I have been thinking about it for the last two hours.' The young monk is surprised and says, 'Brother, I carried that woman in my arms for 15 minutes and you have been carrying her in your mind for the last two hours. Whose sin is bigger?'

Isn't this true for many of us? Carrying the mental baggage of the mistakes we have committed in the past exhausts us. We cannot walk easily with a 10 kilogram bag in each hand. We are bound to feel much lighter if we throw away this load. We cannot laugh at the same joke every day, then how can we cry at the same sorrows for the whole of our lives?

The important question then is: how to throw away this baggage? By repeatedly thinking 'poor me' and 'victim me', what do we achieve? Yes, we unconsciously empathize with ourselves and pamper our ego, and that's why we keep repeating these things. However, these are not empowering thoughts. Understanding this is basically the fundamental step to get rid of these thoughts. Hence, no matter what has happened in the past, by repeating the same thought we cannot grow.

The second kind of past that troubles us is when we carry the guilt of having done somebody wrong, something our conscience finds unpardonable. Why do these incidents trouble us? It is because we have set a very high self-image that is getting scarred because of this. Our dark side was and is also a part of our personality—but it's just a shade of our personality. Everyone has it, and sometimes it comes to the surface. If we accept this, things become simpler. Increasing our kindness and working on being a better version of the self helps. Ultimately, we need to remember that 'every saint has a past and every sinner has a future'.

Those without problems are dead

> *There is only one group of people who do not have problems, and they are all dead. Problems are a sign of life, so the more problems you have, the more alive you are.*
>
> —Norman Vincent Peale[39]

Everyone feels that their problems are the biggest and the most unique. I remember one story. A faith healer goes to a village. People gather around him and ask him the solution to their problems. All of them say that their problems are the biggest and need to be solved on priority. The healer then asks them to write their problems on a piece of paper, folds the slips and bounces them around in a jar. He then distributes the slips of paper randomly, asking them to see if these problems are less serious than the ones they had written. Looking at new problems, everyone starts asking for their previous set of problems because they find that those were less serious.

Our situation is also similar to this. The problems will always be there. Problems could be any and many, but most fall in one or the other of the following categories—financial, physical,

---

[39]Peale, Norman Vincent, QuoteFancy, https://bit.ly/3waWxWd. Accessed on 22 March 2022.

relationship related, success related or death related. And they're all ultimately experienced in one place: in the mind! Basically, the problems which make us helpless are only two: the death of a loved one and a terminal illness striking your body. These two are the toughest problems to handle and require significant counselling. The rest of the problems are not as difficult to handle.

Now how to handle all the above-mentioned problems?

- Try answering the following questions:
  - Is the problem very critical?
  - Will the decision you take to solve this problem be important and relevant for you after five or 10 years?

Deciding the priority of problems is very important because often the tragedy of today is the joke of tomorrow. Defining what exactly the problem is helps in understanding it and drawing attention away from unwanted issues around it.

- Thinking analytically

Dividing the problems into two categories—'under control' and 'beyond control'—helps. Many problems are beyond our control, such as what people think about us or having a child. If it's out of your hands, it deserves freedom from your mind too. Why worry and waste energy in addressing problems beyond your control?

- Are we deriving any implication from a situation which may not be there?

Let's take an example. Suppose I suggest to my spouse that we go for a movie today. He says that he is busy. Tomorrow he has a headache, and the day after that he is not in the mood. What conclusion can I derive from this? That he is avoiding me or I am not that important to him. But can I also just take things at face value? Maybe he really has a headache or is busy or not in the mood. Things become simpler if we don't try to derive hidden implications to simple things.

Stop before you blow your top!

Why do we get angry?
We get angry due to only three reasons:

- Our desire remains unfulfilled;
- Expectations remain unfulfilled;
- We are not allowed to communicate what we wanted to.

Is anger a completely negative emotion? Not really. It's natural to get angry to some extent.

Even history has so many examples of incidents where an insult provoked much anger, which actually resulted in important creations and victories. For example, Saint Tulsidas was madly in love with his wife Ratnavali and was missing her badly when she had gone to her mother's place for a few days. He went to see her in spite of heavy rains, swimming down the river Yamuna for miles. When he reached his mother-in-law's house, his wife opened the door and said sarcastically that she would have been happier if he had shown this dedication in achieving something significant and that he should dedicate this love to God instead of her. Saint Tulsidas turned back at the doorstep and left, beginning his sadhana.

Another example is Guru Chanakya, who was badly insulted for his ugliness by King Dhanananda in a royal ceremony. He channelled his anger into determination and made Chandragupta Maurya the emperor and took revenge for this insult. He channelled the energy of anger and transformed it into inspiration. Limited anger, channelled properly, definitely helps us fight for our rights and safeguard our self-esteem.

What we are worried about is the typical and commonest destructive expression of anger. It requires a few seconds to get angry. When we get angry our blood pressure shoots up, our heart rate increases and we sweat. Sometimes there can be very serious repercussions too. But it takes a lot of time to return to normal in terms of physical and mental parameters. From the human mind's perspective, the events which trigger anger can come with a lot of emotions like irritability, sadness and low self-esteem. All these emotions get even stronger and darker with the mental 'revision' of these incidents. Our ability to work diminishes and we lose a lot of our precious time in the whole process. Also, we end up saying things we don't mean.

So what can we do to control anger? Following small steps helps reduce our anger and its outward expression. Here are a few:

- Consuming a glass of cold water instantaneously reduces anger.
- Before shouting at people, we must ask ourselves three questions:
  i. What I am going to say—is it *good*?
  ii. Is it going to serve any *positive purpose*?
  iii. Is it essential to talk *right now*?

If the answer to any of the above questions is no, then please wait for some time before speaking.

- Write an email to the person with whom you are angry, but don't send it immediately. Once you have finished drafting the email, go for a walk or engage yourself in an activity for a while for distraction. Re-read the email after an hour and edit it if required and then send it if you still want to. This way we avoid the emotional drama which happens in one-to-one fights. Writing also channels our negative energy and we feel better. This method should be used in informal relations, not with your colleagues.

- If an argument is essential, then express your point in an even and calm tone. Respect the other person. Don't use superlatives. Don't use words like 'always' and 'worst'. Avoid abusive language. Talk about the incident alone and don't refer to past occurrences.
- The ancient method of counting up to 100 before uttering a word is also effective.
- Instead of speaking out, if we divert our attention to the bodily changes we are experiencing when we get angry, we calm down easily.
- Humour is magical in these circumstances. When you are angry, remember a joke. It's a strong antidote to anger.
- If we know the 'factors under my control' and the 'factors beyond my control' clearly, then the calculation becomes easy. The behaviour of others, including that of our loved ones, is not in our control. The only things completely in our control are our reactions and expressions of emotions. One must be aware of these things all the time.
- Press the middle finger of your hands for a minute each by encircling it with the fingers of the other hand. This is a well-known acupressure method and many people claim relief from it.
- A good lifestyle—good sleep, good food and daily exercise—is pivotal for a balanced body and mind. Milk is rich in tryptophan, which is responsible for reducing impulsivity, so milk and dairy products should

be included in ample quantities in your diet. When we exercise, endorphins are secreted in the brain. They are natural mood lifters and reduce stress.
- Thought-stopping methods like imagining a stick hitting your head whenever you get negative thoughts helps in reducing unwanted thoughts. Self-hypnosis, progressive muscle-relaxation exercises, breathing exercises and yoga help us control negative emotions and anger.
- Another anger-management technique is praying every day. Prayer cleanses negative emotions and helps us forgive others and ourselves.
- If you feel that the above solutions are not working for you, consult a mental healthcare provider. There are effective medicines for anger management in psychiatry, which can properly address the issue.

Aristotle said, 'Anybody can become angry—that is easy, but to be angry with the right person and to the right degree and at the right time and for the right purpose, and in the right way—that is not within everybody's power and is not easy.' So, it's best to avoid anger altogether. Acknowledging that you are angry is the battle half won.

A goal is your North Star

What do you require to become successful in life? Extraordinary intelligence? Inherited wealth? Educational degrees? Or connect with influential people? Luckily, many a time, you don't need any of these. As aptly put by motivational speaker and author Brian Tracy: 'Your ability to discipline yourself to set clear goals, and then to work towards them every day, will do more to guarantee your success than any other single factor.'

We need goals not only to be successful in life but also for the motivation to get up in the morning. They are the driving force for our daily challenges.

Good goals are necessary for a healthy mind too. People who chase something bigger in life are able to ignore a lot of unimportant and trivial issues in their life. A burning ambition to achieve goals burns all non-value adding and trivial things. So many psychiatric illnesses are prevented as a result. When we achieve set goals, our self-esteem improves too. Irrespective of age, good goals keep our life meaningful and us motivated.

Do goals mean dreams? No, dreams have the colours of desire and hope, but they are shapeless and ill-defined, like a cloud, because they don't have a specific timeframe. So, dreams with well-defined deadlines are goals.

How does one decide goals? Whatever makes us happy and satisfied can be a goal. Most importantly, we need to be attracted to the goals we set. The definition of happiness and satisfaction is different for different people. Hence, other people's goals may not be our goals. This is not something anybody can give you—we need to find our calling. The need and strong desire to achieve them define the success of goals. We need to believe in our goals and we need to believe in powers in the world that support us too.

When we decide our goals, we need to have a holistic view of life. You can decide goals on each and every aspect of life—financial, professional, academic, spiritual, artistic, health and fitness, relationship, social and so on. While forming goals, we should remember every goal has to be a S.M.A.R.T goal, that is, **S** – Specific, **M** – Measurable, **A** – Attainable, **R** – Realistic, **T** – Time-bound.

For example, 'I want to reduce as much weight as possible' is a weak goal. 'I want to reduce 6 kilograms in three months' is specific, measurable, attainable, realistic and time-bound, and hence, it's a strong goal. Similarly, all our goals should be strong goals.

Also, ask yourself: where do I see myself in 10 years? What are your long-term goals? For that, what should you achieve in the coming five years? What should be your goals for the next year and then for the next three years? This helps achieve clarity.

Focus on one goal from each domain at a time. The by-products of that goal could me more. For example, regular exercise reduces weight and is good for keeping your mind happy too. While writing the acclaimed book *Geeta Rahasya*, freedom fighter and philosopher Lokmanya Tilak stopped at one shloka in the Bhagavad Gita: '*Masanam margasheershah aham* (Of the 12 months, I am Margasheershah—the month of November–December)'. Tilak was puzzled as to why Lord Krishna was saying this and started reading up more about it. Thus, other than the *Geeta Rahasya*, he also ended up writing *The Orion*, which is related to antiquity of the Vedas.

Second, goals should be linked to effort and not the outcome. 'I will finish the entire syllabus before the exam and give my best in the exams' is a right goal. But 'I must stand first' should not be a goal, as a lot of factors beyond our control are in play here.

Let your dear ones know about your goals, as they can help keep us motivated and also provide suggestions. Identify the things that waste your time and come in the path of achieving your goals and start working on them. Use creative visualization of fulfilled goals and enjoy the feeling. Reward yourself after the actualization of the goal—after all, we deserve rewards from ourself. In case you are unable to achieve the goal, it's still okay; the journey on that path also teaches us a lot, which, in turn, helps us in redefining the goal. Also, one should remember that as time passes, preference towards certain goals also changes. If some goals don't excite you any more, drop them.

I remember an anonymous quote, 'When I studied human biology, I understood there is not a single cell in the human body which doesn't have any aim however short its lifespan! After reading this, I was surprised by the fact that how my body, made up of millions of cells, could be aimless!' What an awakening statement to form goals and set in action, right?

Overcoming clouds of negativity

We have all faced criticism since childhood and we will face it in the future too. No one can escape this. Why is it important to learn to deal with criticism properly? Our mind starts believing what it hears or what is repeatedly said to it. If someone repeatedly says you are mad, not good for anything, then after a few repetitions, your mind will accept it and you will feel the same about yourself. So it's important to 'mind' what you hear.

When patients tell me, 'Doctor, people tell me I am not good, that I am a loser!', I ask them, 'Don't tell me what others think about you, tell me what you think about yourself'. Often, we don't think independently for ourselves, and what people say about us becomes our reality.

We pay more attention to the negative comments coming our way, and tend to sideline the positive ones. In fact, if someone says something positive aloud, like, 'Oh beautiful, look here', we may not turn around because we assume that it is not for us. But if someone says something like, 'You fool!' in public, we will typically turn back to see if it was addressed to us.

It always boils down to us and what we decide to accept about ourselves, never about others. Mentally, we keep reiterating so many negative things about ourselves every day! The conscious mind is a thinker, the unconscious is a prover.

If you think that you are good for nothing, the unconscious mind will try to prove you are right.

So, what can be done to improve your reaction to others' criticism, to enhance your self-esteem and improve your self-dialogue? Whenever you face any criticism, analyse if it's provided from a point of view of improvement. In other words, see if it is constructive. If you see that there is some point in it, try to improve yourself based on this feedback. If you feel it was pointless and done only from a point of view of pulling you down, ignore it.

Don't allow those negative comments or criticism to linger in your mind if you find that they are pointless. How can you do that? Imagine, I want to gift you a book. You say, 'I don't want it.' With whom does the book remain? With me, right? Similarly, if you refuse to accept negative comments, they remain with the person who made the comment.

Do write down your achievements. I don't mean just academic or athletic achievements here—those are definitely big things, but also those difficult and challenging times that you handled well. Those are your self-esteem boosters, and each of us has many of such instances. Do read these achievements again and again.

Reduce contact with negative people, people who have a problem with everything. Trust me, you will feel better. If you cannot avoid such people who criticize you baselessly (say, because he is your boss or a relative), then try to create emotional distance with them by not taking their comments seriously.

Love yourself first

If I ask you to name any three people you love most, most would answer parents, partner and child. How many of you would take your own name? I am sure not many. How many of us feel we are not good enough? Or that we are a failure? Or don't feel good after looking in the mirror?

If your answer to any of these questions is a yes, how can we expect others to love or respect us? If we feel we are not good enough, that we are not worthy of good things and respect, people will mirror that thought.

The solution: self-love and self-appreciation.

What it is like loving yourself

Self-love means accepting your strengths, your weaknesses and everything in between.

It does not mean narcissism or delusional self-love, like saying 'I am the most intelligent person in the class'. It is accepting your strengths and weaknesses. It is about loving yourself with the understanding that some of the not-so-good traits in our personality can be changed quickly, some will take longer and some perhaps will never change.

How do you love your child? How do you love your parents? We know they are not perfect, they have issues, just like everyone else, but we love them nevertheless. Similarly, we need to love ourselves.

Is it important to love and appreciate yourself? Why?

Imagine yourself in a relationship with someone you don't love, don't appreciate and still have no option but to live with them. How does this make you feel?

I remember Kareena Kapoor's famous dialogue from *Jab We Met*: '*Main apni favourite hun!* (I am my favourite!)'. In the first-half of the movie, we see the self-loving version of her, which is a girl full of life and energy. She's so happy that her happiness rubs off on Aditya Kashyap (played by Shahid Kapoor), who is going through a rough patch, after a break-up and incurring financial losses, and is planning on ending his life. She brings him back to normalcy. In the second half, we see the depressed version of the heroine, full of doubts and regrets. Which version do we love? Obviously, the first one.

Self-appreciation has many benefits: good mental health, better quality of relationships, success in major endeavours, social effectiveness and better coping with failures.

What are the simple ways to love and appreciate yourself?

I love one very famous method introduced by the American author and motivational speaker Louise Hay called the 'Mirror Method'. Often what we say to ourselves is pretty negative and causes great harm to our self-esteem in the long run and could even be a harbinger of depression. However we can learn to appreciate ourselves for whatever we are and accept ourselves for who we are! After waking up in the morning, the first thing we should do is stand in front of the mirror, smile, take our name and say, 'I love you, I accept you the way you are!' It's pretty simple, but a very effective method.

Say nice things about yourself throughout the day whenever you get the time. It could be simple statements like, 'This dress suits me; I am looking pretty', or 'What an intelligent decision I took in today's meeting'. Keep on pleasing the inner child in you.

If something goes wrong or you make a mistake, ask yourself if you have learnt a lesson from it. If the answer is yes, then don't keep on punishing yourself in your head. In fact, tell yourself, 'It's okay, I am learning, this is just one mistake and it doesn't define me. I am fine and can perform well.' Don't you think this is a better way to handle things? Till now, we have criticized ourselves, so can we try to acknowledge, appreciate and encourage ourselves? Ultimately what really matters is what you think about yourself, and once that dialogue is improved, things become good in life.

Power of positive thinking

According to the famous psychiatrist and psychoanalyst Sigmund Freud, this world and every living being in this world is run by two kinds of energies: Eros and Thanatos. Eros is the energy for life—positive energy, whereas Thanatos is the energy which pulls all living beings towards death—destructive energy. The universe tries to balance these energies. The positive productive energy dominates in birds, animals, nature and wherever there is life. The human body and mind can be exceptions to this. Our brain is more evolved and consequently our thoughts are more evolved than other animals' as well. So, we have the power to choose our thoughts. However, negative thoughts come to the mind more often than positive thoughts, and there are reasons for that too. Negative thinking is very easy and spontaneous as opposed to positive thinking, for which we have to make an effort. Negative thoughts originate in fear, anger and jealousy and from a fatalistic attitude like blaming major events on bad luck. In contrast, positive thoughts originate from hopefulness, willpower and the belief that we can do something to change the situation. As the famous saying goes, 'We become what we think!'

Although negative thinking is easy, it's very dangerous. Our negative thinking is responsible to a large extent for whatever sadness and unfortunate events we have attracted in our life. So, it's very important to uplift our thoughts by making an effort to think positive.

In the Indian context, we have age-old guidance on what

we should think and what we should not. From the verses of the Bhagavad Gita and literature by Saint Tukaram and Saint Ramdas, to the writings of recent western philosophers such as Neale Donald Walsch and Rhonda Byrne, all have given more importance to our thoughts than our actual deeds. How come they are all in synchrony regarding this? Deeds, acts and how we behave are definitely important, but the thought behind those acts decides whether that act is good or bad. Also, our mind, from where the thoughts originate, is a big electromagnetic powerhouse. We attract the same kind of thought vibrations as we emit. Those vibrations become powerful and slowly other forces in the universe too act to reaffirm those thoughts. So, if we are at the centre of this powerful process, if we meditate on something we want, we will get it. If we meditate on the fact that something must not happen, you attract that as well. After all, focusing on that energy gives result.

So, let's try to focus on the things we want, and not on the things that we don't want. We can do that by following these steps:

- Make a list of things that make you happy. There is a strong connection between a feeling of happiness and positivity. The things that make others happy may not make you happy. In that case, pursuing the things which you don't truly like may not bring happiness. From that personal list of happiness, take responsibility to fulfil your dreams and goals. Use creative imagery to bring more positivity about achieving those.
- Devote five minutes every morning to recalling things you are grateful for: good health, a roof over your head, enough food, financial independence, and most importantly, your family and friends. If we are grateful,

we feel positive and attract positivity.
- Complain less. When it's essential, do complain—don't accept injustice. But don't complain to others for petty issues and don't complain in your mind either.
- Avoid unhealthy patterns of gossips. If we gossip a lot, our energy gets wasted in all the wrong things.
- Try to help at least one person in a day. We have been helped by several people in our life on multiple occasions. We don't even know the names of many of these people, neither do we remember their faces. But we do remember those small acts of kindness. I remember the quote by William Wordsworth: 'The best portion of a good man's life: his little, nameless unremembered acts of kindness and love.' We all have kindness and love inside us, and we simply need to use it often. For example, you can buy grocery for the old people in your neighbourhood, offer water to the delivery boy or guide someone while they are parking the car. Simple, small acts of kindness add happiness and satisfaction to our life.
- Discuss your issues only with a select few. Most people won't be able to offer a solution, and by repeating the issues to multiple people, we get more mentally entangled in those problems.
- Before going to bed, try to recall the *best* thing that happened that day and express your gratefulness for it.

Live well to feel well

One of the most important yet neglected areas is our lifestyle. Recently, I came across a meme—two ticket windows were shown, one for instant results by consuming pills which had a costly ticket, second for lifestyle changes for long-term relief at a very nominal cost. A long queue of people was at the pills counter and the other counter had not even opened the account. We all want instant results with minimal efforts but it's not always possible. For long-term results in our overall health, we need to invest in lifestyle changes.

As per Ayurveda, the most important factors that decide if the lifestyle is good or bad are the trisutras: ahara (proper nutrition), vihara (lifestyle) and nidra (sleep). All three are of paramount importance in governing our physical as well as mental well-being.

For our diet, we should follow the 80:20 rule. That is, have 80 per cent clean diet in a week and 20 per cent cheat meals, such as fried foods and sweets for cravings. A diet that is very high in refined sugars increases the jitteriness of the mind. We ask parents to reduce sweet foods for paediatric patients with attention-deficit/hyperactivity disorder (ADHD), as sweets increase hyperactivity and inattention. Try to cut excess salt in the diet as well, particularly if facing excessive fluid retention in the body. Salt should be avoided particularly by women who are facing premenstrual blues for a week before their menstruation starts, as it definitely reduces irritability.

As said correctly, food is the most abused anxiety drug. Exercise is the most underutilized antidepressant. The WHO recommends 30 minutes of moderate-intensity aerobic exercise five days a week for adults and 60 minutes of aerobic exercise for children. In addition to routine benefits to the body, like lowering the risk of cardiorespiratory illnesses and certain cancers and improving stamina, daily cardio exercise is good for your mental health too. With just 20 minutes of brisk walking, your negative energy and anxiety gets channelled and endorphins (which are natural mood lifters) are secreted in the mind. Any exercise that increases your heart rate is good for your mind too. So, take up brisk walking, running, jogging or cycling.

Here, it's important to distinguish between exertion and exercise. Many of my patients say, 'I work a lot at home, do I still need to exercise?' Yes, we all need to exercise, regardless of how much we exert in a day. What we do mechanically is not rhythmic. I don't deny its physiological benefits, but exercise is when we dedicate specific time for it and do it rhythmically for a significant period of time with a relaxed mind. It is way more effective for your mind and body than pure exertion. It's better to walk in the open air like on a walking track or in a park than in an isolated environment like a home gym. When you see trees, plants, flowers and children playing around and hear the chirping of birds, your mood is instantly uplifted, breaking the monotony and drudgery of life.

It's said that almost 30 per cent of the world's population suffers from insomnia,[40] i.e. out of every 100 people, 30 get insufficient sleep or have disturbed sleep or feel a lack of freshness after getting up in the morning for at least three days in a week. Such a high prevalence of sleeplessness, right! We need sound sleep to provide good rest to mind and body; sleep rejuvenates almost all organs in the body, helps in better immune function and increases our productivity. Sleep is overall a mirror of our health. When anyone comes to us with disturbed sleep, we ask about mental stressors as well as bodily issues. Sleep gets affected in case of major disturbances in either. Also, disturbed sleep can itself cause mental disturbances such as irritability, lethargy, low moods,

---

[40] Roth, Thomas, 'Insomnia: Definition, Prevalence, Etiology, and Consequences', *Journal of Clinical Sleep Medicine*, 15 August 2007; 3 (5 Suppl): S7–S10, https://bit.ly/37DGFkO. Accessed on 17 March 2022.

absent-mindedness, etc. While evaluating, we need to consider and evaluate sleep disturbances carefully, as it could be both the cause and effect of disturbances of the mind.

Most of us need six to eight hours of sleep, although there are some short sleepers, who need very little sleep, say four to five hours.

For good sleep, we need to follow sleep hygiene and discipline, which is basically a collection of habits that promote good and sound sleep. These are as follows:

- Fix a time to go to bed and wake up. Follow this for most days. This sets a biorhythm, and we don't face difficulty falling asleep once we get habituated to this cycle.
- The bed should be used only for sleeping and not for chatting, talking over the phone, playing with gadgets, watching television, reading or eating. This is very important, because if we use the bed only for sleeping, it will act as a conditioning mechanism such that when we lie down on the bed, the mind automatically gets a signal that it's time to sleep.
- If you are not getting sleep in spite of lying in bed for 30 minutes, then instead of tossing and turning in bed, go in some other room and start working quietly or read something till you feel sleepy again.
- Have a high-tryptophan snack like a cup of warm milk or a cheese slice 30 minutes before going to bed. Milk products are rich in the neurotransmitter tryptophan, which is a sleep precursor hormone.
- Taking a warm shower two to three hours prior to bedtime also helps.
- You should schedule your exercise for the morning and not after 5.00 p.m.

- Meals should be taken at least two hours prior to sleep.
- Tea or coffee should not be taken after 5.00 p.m. Caffeine keeps the mind stimulated for a long time and sleep initiation can be a problem.
- The bedroom should be conducive to sleep. Avoid exposure to loud noise and bright lights an hour prior to bedtime. Clean/washed and light-coloured bedsheets help in better sleep. A temperature between 22 and 28 degree Celsius is best for sound sleep.

A few other important lifestyle changes which should be implemented in our routine are:

- Make time for family and friends.
  Have one meal a day at the table with your family. This is an excellent way to find out how everyone's day went and keep the bond within the family intact. It can also keep everyone healthy and away from substance abuse. Plan an annual vacation with the family, as this can be a great opportunity to create fond memories. Scheduling an outing with your family once a month is also an excellent way to connect with everyone. Even a half-day trip can be very rejuvenating and can break the monotony. To spend more time with your parents, pick up a hobby together. You may enjoy cooking a meal together or gardening. Have a list of friends you will always call to wish on a birthday.
- Make time for yourself. This time could be very helpful for introspection and reflection.
- Keep some time to organize and schedule your time. This reduces a lot of confusion and mental clutter. Use a diary, calendar or Google Sheets to track your personal and professional commitments. Delegate all tasks that

you have been doing for the longest time and look around to see who can do it for you. We get angry often because someone did not do what we thought they should. Communicating clearly and asking people to remember tasks helps.
- Inculcate a hobby and dedicate time for it. It acts as an excellent detox. Also, creativity keeps us happy and channels our anxiety into productivity.

Run your day!

'Either run the day or the day runs you!' What an apt statement about time management by the American entrepreneur, author and motivational speaker Jim Rohn. A lot of stress and dissatisfaction in life comes from poor time management skills. Many successful and happy people say that the key to success is good time management. The question is: how to achieve that? This wonderful grid is quite helpful.

	URGENT	NOT URGENT
IMPORTANT	DO *Do it now*	DECIDE *Schedule a time to do it*
NOT IMPORTANT	DELEGATE *Who can do it for you?*	DELETE *Eliminate it*

First quadrant: Things which are important and urgent need to be taken care of right away. These could be your professional commitments, a health check-up or investing the amount in a fixed deposit that has matured (by the way, good management of finances is the key to reducing a variety of stressors).

Second quadrant: When it comes to things which are important but not urgent, decide on a deadline and schedule some time for it. For example: getting a passport issued/renewed or learning to drive.

Third quadrant: For the things which are important but urgent, delegate the responsibility to someone who is capable of handling it. These things have urgency of time but they don't necessarily need your presence or involvement. For example, ironing your clothes or cleaning your room.

Fourth quadrant: Get rid of the things which are neither important nor urgent. These could be potential time wasters, such as installing unwanted apps on your mobile.

One more category which is not mentioned in the grid but can potentially be very important for all of us is 'not urgent but like to do'. If we manage the grid of the four quadrants properly, we will get some time to do the things which are not urgent but which we like to do and which are linked with our pleasure principle. Examples of these could be taking out time to spend with our children, for our hobbies or to learn a new skill.

In this scheduling, don't forget to include me-time in the important-but-not-urgent domain. Simple things like smelling your coffee and reflecting on life to enjoying a long, warm shower and going for long walks alone can actually help us hear our inner voice, which usually gets drowned in the dissonance of our everyday life.

One more principle which I find very important for time management and stress reduction is learning to say no. Identifying the situations where you need to assertively say no really changes the equation of time management. We often find it difficult to say no, maybe due to the influence of the other person, our own shy nature, a perceived obligation or a lack of clarity, but it often generates more friction in our thoughts and more resistance in our mind when we don't want to do something but still *have* to do it. We spend a lot of time battling these thoughts and doing the thing unwillingly. We can stop this vicious cycle by learning to say no in an assertive and firm but polite manner.

Some quick fixes

When we feel stressed, we can try the below-mentioned instant stress busters. Though the effects are short-lived, they offer relief when we are involved in some important tasks—such as appearing for an important exam or interview, or making a crucial presentation—and need to be in the best frame of mind.

Stress-busting methods using our five senses:

- **Vision**
  - Gazing at an aquarium for a few minutes
  - Visiting a nature park
  - Wearing the colour blue as it brings a feeling of calmness, security, tranquillity and positivity
- **Hearing**
  - Listening to soothing music
  - Listening to classical ragas such as Bhairav, Pooriya or Dhanashree
- **Taste**
  - Eating a piece of dark chocolate
  - Having a cup of coffee
  - Drinking a glass of warm milk
  - Munching on a fistful of nuts

- **Touch**
  - Taking acupressure
  - Playing with a pet
  - Having a warm bath
  - Walking barefoot on grass
- **Smell**
  - Smelling roses
  - Applying essential oils, such as lavender

Some other methods that work equally well are:

- Clenching your hands and releasing them
- Sharing with loved ones
- Decluttering your workspace
- Listing things that make you happy
- Recalling pleasant memories
- Playing the flute
- Inflating a balloon
- Praying
- Watching funny videos or reading jokes
- Practising deep breathing
- Practising mindfulness meditation
- Brisk walking

There are some over-the-counter (OTC) drugs that you can take, such as vitamin C tablets and ashwagandha.

Stress is going to be a part of our life, particularly the kind of life we live nowadays in cities. However, if we are able to control them, build our resilience, understand the factors that are under our control and those that are not, regularly practise the above-mentioned simple solutions, follow a healthy lifestyle, channel our energy in productive ways and train our mind to think in the right way, we can certainly reduce the likelihood of depression. It is important to remember that these solutions are not foolproof in preventing depression in cases where genetic and endogenous factors are strongly operating, but they can definitely help to reduce the distress which is a precursor of reactionary depression. Ultimately, the power lies in our reactions, our responses, and we will be able to control these if we train our mind. It is worth remembering that we can not always choose what happens to us, but we can always choose our response to it.

6
I CAN BE CURED

'Doctor, let me tell you, reaching a psychiatrist is often a long journey, where the first major roadblock is that we don't understand depression well, so it's a lost road, like going in a lost direction. So much time goes in trying to find out what exactly is wrong with us. Then there are cobwebs of misunderstandings about its treatment, misconceptions which misguide us. And finally when we track our way out to reach the right door, it's invariably late and we have already gone through a great deal of suffering!'

This was the answer one of my patients of depression gave to my question about why he suffered for so long time without any treatment.

A patient faces many roadblocks before actually coming for the treatment for depression. They may feel:

- 'People will be judgmental towards me, may feel pity for me or may make fun of me.'
- 'Maybe it's just a bad phase. Does depression really exist?'
- 'People around me were never supportive of treatment for depression and were always saying it's just in the head or you are simply giving excuses.'
- 'I am scared that my diagnosis will define me. I don't

want to get labelled with my psychiatric diagnosis.'
- 'I have not heard positive things about treatment for depression, basically about antidepressants. I want to stay away from it and give myself one more chance to work on myself.'

When it comes to treatments for depression, yes, identifying that there's a problem and acknowledging it forms the first step. Second is getting rid of all the myths associated with depression. Starting the actual treatment is the final step.

We should come out of the shell of denial and shyness and move ahead with the treatment as early as possible for a number of reasons. A few have been listed below:

- Contrary to popular belief, accepting the fact that you require assistance in the current situation is actually a matter of courage and not weakness.
- If treated at the right time, depression is easily curable. Waiting for a long period increases the severity of depression and takes longer to cure.
- When you are depressed, you may appear to be a solo traveller on this lonely road, but that's not the case. There are many others who are suffering, and if you take the treatment, take lessons from it and share your story, others too will share theirs and we will be able to curb this pandemic of depression, which is the major contributor to psychological morbidity.

Your illness doesn't define you, but your strength and courage do. And your story can inspire others. So, break the pattern and be an inspiration.

Myths versus facts

Let us now address the myths associated with depression, and treatment as a second step to managing it.

Myth: Once you start taking antidepressants, you have to take them forever. In fact, any psychiatric illness is forever.

Fact: Not all medical disorders like common cold and infection require treatment for life. We just finish a standard course and then we are done. A few diseases like diabetes, hypertension, and hypothyroidism may require treatment for life.

Similarly, in many cases like unipolar depression[41], anxiety, and sexual and sleep disorders, medicines are normally given for a specific duration and withdrawn gradually.

In some psychiatric disorders like schizophrenia and bipolar disorder, medicines are given for life because these disorders typically last for life, just like diabetes, and the continuing treatment is given in the best interest of the patient so they can lead a normal life.

Myth: Antidepressants come with side effects.

Fact: Every medication has some side effects. For example: taking simple B-complex tablet will give you foul-smelling burps. Psychiatric medicines are not devoid of side effects, but the majority of them are very mild and often self-limiting. They start within a couple of days and disappear or reduce in a couple of weeks. Similarly, the effects of the medicine are as large as a pumpkin and the side effects are the size of peanuts in comparison, hence they should not prevent you from taking

---

[41]Unipolar means where only depression is present, which is not a part of bipolar depression and no other complicating factors are present.

the medicines if your psychiatrist prescribes them.

Myth: Self-help methods like yoga, exercise, reading positive books and alternate treatments are quite effective and should be tried first.

Fact: No doubt these are preventive strategies, but a depressed brain is beyond the reach of these methods most of the time, barring cases of very mild depression. So, we recommend them in maintenance regimen in the treatment of depression along with the ongoing medicines or as lifestyle strategies in preventing further episodes of depression and managing stress effectively.

Myth: Antidepressants are not the solution to depression—although they make you feel better, once you stop them, your symptoms return.

Fact: If you take medicines for infection, you may feel better within 48 hours. However, if you stop the medicines without finishing the prescribed course, the infection may not completely clear from your body and may return.

Similarly, in spite of feeling completely fine, the medicines are given for maintenance course to prevent the recurrence of symptoms. After the standard course is over, we gradually reduce the dosage and then discontinue it as a whole. In such cases, patients don't experience any discomfort and do absolutely fine after discontinuing the course.

Myth: You won't ever be able to discontinue taking your psychiatric medicines because when you do, you get a flu-type illness.

Fact: These are called 'withdrawal symptoms', which comprise flu-like feelings, body pains, strange sensations in the body and general feelings of discomfort. They come when any medicine being taking for some months is abruptly stopped, as your brain has got habituated to its effects. It's not an addiction, as you don't tend to increase the dose on your own, which is the distinguishing feature of an addiction. It's just a withdrawal effect that can happen with many other medicines for physical illnesses as well.

The solution to this is that we taper off the medicine very slowly. Your brain knows the difference between 100 kilograms in one hand and 50 kilograms in the other, but it doesn't understand the difference if you put 100 kilograms in one hand and 99.5 kilograms in the other hand. The distinction is very subtle. While lowering the dosage of the medicines, we use the same principle, and patients normally don't face any problem when we taper off and eventually stop the medicines.

Myth: Antidepressants make you sleepy and are addictive.

Fact: If taken under the supervision of a psychiatrist, nothing is addiction forming. It's self-medication which may give rise to addiction and abuse. Not only antidepressants, but many drugs used in other areas of medicine have the potential for abuse and addiction, such as painkillers used for inflammation in the body. Over-the-counter antidiarrheal medicines like imodium and butylscopolamine are also abused by some patients.

Some antidepressants cause sleepiness and some don't. In fact, we give some antidepressants in the morning, as they energize you. In addition to using antidepressants, if the patient is not getting sleep, which is a major problem in many patients in the early run of the treatment, we have to prescribe medicines to induce sleep for a brief duration for the patient's comfort. Once the depression starts to settle, the sleep pattern automatically improves and we can withdraw the sleeping pills, usually within two to four weeks.

Myth: Psychiatric medicines should be avoided and counselling should be taken as far as possible.

Fact: Neither are we eager to start medicines for depression, nor do all patients need psychiatry medicines. Some get better through counselling, diet and exercise and other forms of psychotherapy.

However, recovery depends on multiple factors such as the severity and duration of the symptoms, other illnesses complicating the case, significant family history, the number of depression episodes and so on.

In severe depression, which lasts for a longer duration or causes multiple episodes and other illnesses, initially the mind is not in a position to accept psychotherapy. We need to use antidepressants for some time to put the mind at ease, and then as per the patient's choices and clinical picture, we can take the next call.

Myth: Antidepressants may curb your creativity, make you numb and change your basic nature and personality.

Fact: It's the depression that curbs creativity when it gets severe, although people with milder depression write and paint quite well, especially on the negative aspects of life.[42] They have difficulty in expressing the other shade of life in their creations, and as the depression advances, the person's creative thinking also gets blocked and their activities and thinking slow down. Antidepressants bring the mood and thoughts back to normal, and a person can enjoy life with more interest. The patient's personality or nature is more or less a constant thing and is usually not altered with antidepressants.

---

[42] Andreasen, Nancy C., 'The relationship between creativity and mood disorders', *Dialogues Clin Neurosci.*, June 2008, 10(2): 251–55, https://bit.ly/3xhHryJ. Accessed on 12 April 2022.

Myth: Saying 'Keep calm and cheer yourself' to the depressed person is a useful practice.

Fact: Just as by saying 'Control your sugar intake and blood pressure level' a person cannot control it, similarly by scolding a depressed person for their depression or just asking them to be cheerful doesn't serve any purpose.

Myth: Depression doesn't need any treatment and can be cured over the course of time.

Fact: In very few cases and at a milder severity, a single episode of depression may get cured of its own in a few months or with the help of a diet (particularly one rich in tryptophan and antioxidants) and a good aerobic exercise regime. However, the majority of the cases need to be managed by a mental healthcare provider. In fact, approaching a psychiatrist earlier increases the chance of complete remission or cure. If the person decides to wait and the depression becomes chronic, some changes may happen in the brain structures and neurotransmitters which may require a longer and more complex treatment.

Myth: Antidepressants increase appetite and cause weight gain.

Fact: Some antidepressants increase appetite, and we choose them in patients who face appetite loss due to depression. There are some antidepressants which don't have any effect on appetite—in fact, they mostly reduce appetite and are chosen when indicated.

Myth: Antidepressants may affect your sex life.

Fact: Depression as well as some antidepressants may affect a patient's sex life. As a result of depression, patients by and large report a reduction of sexual desire and performance too, as depression makes you less interested in previously pleasurable activities. Many patients actually report greater sexual desire after starting antidepressants and as the depression lifts. However, we cannot deny that some antidepressants come with sexual side effects, but these effects are temporary and can be very well managed by talking to your treating doctor, who can adjust the dose, add a new drug or replace the drug with side effects with some other medicines.

Myth: Human beings think and feel for themselves and a pill can't alter anyone's thought processes or emotions.

Fact: Not just a pill, even what you eat as regular food influences your thought process. It's proved beyond doubt that excessive sugar makes you jittery, excessive coffee makes you feel anxious, your thoughts race and even make you sleepless, and a good amount of milk promotes good sleep and feelings of overall well-being. A pill is more potent and targeted to specific changes intended in depression. When simple dietary changes or a good exercise regime can make you feel positive, then how come a pill won't? It has to, right? Every neurotransmitter in the right amount plays a good role in maintaining the right framework of mind, and balancing its evils definitely alters the way you think and feel.

Myth: You shouldn't open up to a mental healthcare provider as they can share that information with your friends and family.

Fact: Confidentiality is the patient's right and no psychiatrist breaches that barring two situations, where privileged communications may be allowed.

    i.   If the patient is suicidal or homicidal, the psychiatrist may share the relevant details with the caretaker of the patient to ensure safety.

ii. If asked, we need to give all the details in the court of law.

Other than these two cases, nothing can be revealed without the patient's consent.

Myth: Psychiatrists can read your mind and may read the things which you are uncomfortable sharing.

Fact: We may be better than others at reading a person's behaviour and understanding their mental state and personality, but we cannot read a person's thoughts unless they speak up about themself or give some behavioural cues.

Whom to consult?

Now coming to the actual treatment for depression, whom should one consult for treatment of depression? A counsellor? A psychologist? Or a psychiatrist?

Many people are confused about this; in fact, many people don't know the difference between these three entities.

A counsellor can be anyone who has done basic courses in psychological counselling.

A psychologist normally has an MPhil, a PhD or an MSc in psychology. They conduct psychotherapy sessions, and some of them are trained to conduct tests for intelligence quotient (IQ), personality, etc.

A psychiatrist is a medical doctor who undergoes training in psychiatry after their MBBS degree. They can diagnose and treat all major and minor mental disorders, conduct psychotherapy, prescribe medications and advise hospitalization, and conduct special procedures like electroconvulsive therapy (ECT), transcranial magnetic stimulation and lie detector tests.

The question is: which of these three is to be consulted?

Ideally, a psychiatrist should be consulted, as they can diagnose the condition deeply and decide the plan of action. A psychiatrist is trained to conduct all kinds of therapy in addition to prescribing medicines. Sometimes the complaint for which a patient comes in is superficial and the actual problem could be something totally different. For example, many people who come with anger issues have underlying depression, which makes them sensitive to petty issues leading to anger dysregulation. In marital therapy as well, if either of the partner is suffering from a major mental illness such as excessive suspiciousness on the partner resulting from paranoid personality problem or paranoid schizophrenia, which is causing a rift in the relationship, it needs to be addressed first. For assessment, meeting a psychiatrist is highly recommended.

However, in a country like India, there is one psychiatrist for 3,500 people, so there is a dearth of psychiatrists. Meeting a psychiatrist for every small or big mental health issue may not be always feasible. Second, although all of us are trained in psychotherapy, the majority of us don't have the time to conduct exclusive psychotherapy or counselling for our patients, although most of us use psychotherapeutic methods and counselling tips in our 30–40-minute sessions in addition to prescribing medicines, which are quite helpful for common psychiatric conditions. And the majority of counsellors and psychologists have an overview of major mental illnesses and they refer the cases beyond their domain or for co-management to psychiatrists.

Therefore, broadly speaking, if someone is facing marital issues or parenting issues, talking to a counsellor can be helpful. If there are internal conflicts about the present situation, the past or about childhood traumas, then talking to a psychologist makes sense. In addition to the conditions mentioned above, if the patient is suffering from frequent breakdowns due to any cause or having difficulties in day-to-day functioning for any reasons, talking to a psychiatrist should be the solution.

Psychotherapy and/or medicines?

Another frequently asked question is whether a patient should go for therapy or for medications.

I would suggest discussing this question with your treating doctor who is making your case profile, as each case is different. But below are the general guidelines for when we should consider medicines and when we should consider psychotherapy.

Medicines form the mainstay of treatment in the following case scenarios:

- When a patient is facing severe depression
- When comorbid illnesses like anxiety and addictions complicate the depression
- Family history of depression and
- Chronic depression

When in a heightened emotional state due to severe depression, no counselling can reach the patient's mind. I remember a quote by American television host and author Fred Rogers: 'There are times when explanations, no matter how reasonable, just don't seem to help!' So, it's not that the patient doesn't understand what you are telling them but the depression is so overwhelming that the thoughts of hopelessness, helplessness and worthlessness return in some time and they feel powerless.

Second, any form of talk therapy takes eight to 10 weeks on an average to show a demonstrable change in depression, whereas with medications, you see changes in a couple of weeks with better control over symptoms as per the requirement of the patients.

Therapy requires patience and time commitment towards sessions as well as homework, which may not be convenient for many patients.

The advantages of cognitive behavioural therapy (CBT) or any other talk therapy are:

- No systemic effects; medication may have side effects on the body
- With therapy, a person may develop strategies and ways to combat depression which eventually may help them combat problems arising later in life

However, counselling and talk therapy can be combined with medications for best results. In fact, the majority of psychiatrists use talk therapy in addition to medicines in their standard 30–40-minute session. Most of the time, it's not a choice between either exclusive counselling or medications. It's normally medications plus therapy. We all know that a very mild case of diabetes can be managed with lifestyle changes such as a low-carbohydrate diet clubbed with a good exercise regimen, but if the sugars in the blood are high, we need to use both medications and lifestyle measures to get things under control. So, if a person comes in the distress state, which comes before the actual disease depression state, we may be able to manage the case with counselling or therapy.

Distress is where mind and body are not in harmony, stress symptoms such as frequently disturbed mood, easy irritability and feelings of pressure and stress are present, and there is susceptibility to catching physical illnesses like cold and cough. However, the person is still able to function normally in their social and occupational sphere, meaning that although they are still fulfilling their family responsibilities and are able to meet deadlines in their professional sphere, albeit with some difficulty, the characteristic and sufficient features of depression are not present. In other words, they are yet to experience ideas of hopelessness, helplessness, worthlessness or socio-occupational deterioration. Therapy and counselling can halt the depression at the distress stage if used properly, but once the depression state establishes itself with sufficient severity, medications are needed to control it and gradually therapy sessions are introduced.

We use exclusive talk therapy or counselling in milder forms of depression, such as with relationship issues. Let's understand a little more about one of the most popular talk therapy—CBT.

Cognitive behaviour therapy (CBT)

CBT or 'cognitive behaviour therapy' is one of the most effective forms of talking therapy used in the management of depression and anxiety. Cognitive behaviour therapy is based on the principal that it is not a situation that influences our feelings and behaviours, but our perception or thoughts regarding the situation.

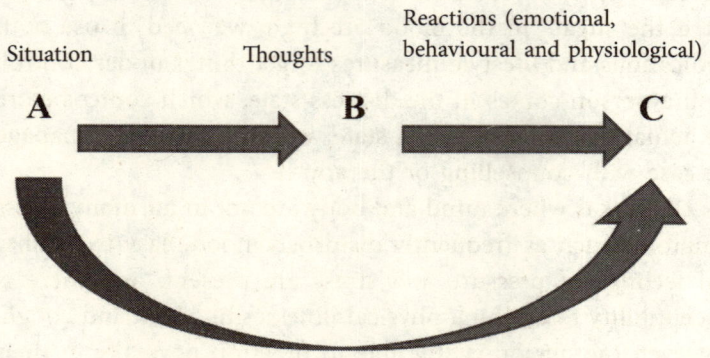

If A is a situation, C our behaviour or reaction to the situation, what we typically think is that A leads to C. However, there is a significant point B, comprising our thoughts and perceptions, which influences C.

Let's take an example. Imagine you are walking by and you see a friend. You wave at him but he does not wave back. How will you feel? Angry, frustrated, sad? What will be the thoughts going through in your head? 'He is ignoring me', 'I must have done something wrong' or 'He must not behave this rudely'. On the other hand, you can think that 'He might have not seen me' or 'He must be busy'. Depending on your thinking, you may feel irritated or neutral about the same situation. Your subsequent behaviour with your friend will also be influenced by your perception about this situation. So, it is our thoughts that determine our emotions and behaviour and not the situation or events in our life.

Thoughts

We usually tend to consider our thoughts as absolute. It is important to understand that our thoughts are a product of our brain functioning and are created by certain neurobiological processes in our brain. Thoughts are mere opinions, not facts. What we think and believe is based on our own perceptions. Had it been a fact and absolute truth, everyone would think in a similar way. For example, the sun rises in the east is a fact, but that the east is the most auspicious direction as the sun rises in the east is just an opinion.

The below table summarizes the difference between facts and opinions.

Facts	Opinions
Can be verified	Based on a perception
Can be supported by evidence	Not necessarily supported by evidence
'Pink is a colour.'	'Pink is the best colour.'
'Some species of tortoise and turtles cannot be legally owned in India.'	'We should not keep turtles and tortoise as pets.'

Each one of us has a distinct thinking style which makes our actions and behaviours predictable. If you are late to work, you can predict how your boss will react. You know how your spouse will respond if you go on a shopping spree. It's because we think and respond predictably. Our thinking pattern is determined by numerous factors, such as genetics, past experiences and our current mental state.

It is usually a combination of all these factors that determine your thinking style.

Here are some examples of an unhealthy thinking style:

- **Catastrophizing**: Assuming the worse in each situation. For example, a woman assumes her husband has met with an accident when he is late from work.
- **Black-and-white thinking**: Looking at everything as either good or bad without any scope of a grey area. For example, we might think that a friend did not help because she is a selfish person.
- **Overgeneralization**: Seeing a pattern based on very little data. For example, a person who was cheated once believes that people can never be trusted.
- **Labelling**: Putting a tag on yourself and others. For example, you might think you are a failure after failing just one exam.
- **Magnification and minimization**: Exaggerating the

negatives in us and downplaying the positives. For example, a student who qualifies for the baseball team may attribute her selection to good luck and blame herself for losing the game after missing a shot.
- **Jumping to conclusions**: Making predictions about other people's thoughts (mind-reading) and predictions about the future (fortune-telling). For example, after a presentation that did not go very well, you might think that everyone must be making fun of you behind your back.
- **Personalization**: Considering yourself responsible for a negative event, often leading to guilt and shame. For example, a parent might believe that it is their fault that their child did not score well in a test and that they should have worked harder and given them more time and attention.
- **Mental filter or selective abstraction**: This is the tendency to ignore the positives and focus exclusively on the negatives. For example, you might think, 'I could not finish the last assignment given to me today. This is the worst day of my life.'
- **Emotional reasoning**: Gauging the truth on the basis of your feelings. For example: 'I must have done something wrong as I feel guilty all the time.'

The good news is that just as you can learn a certain way of thinking, you can also unlearn it. This is the same way that an Indian who has moved to the US initially finds it difficult to follow right-hand driving but gradually gets used to it. It is possible to adapt a different way of thinking with practise.

Thoughts versus feelings

Let's understand the difference between our thoughts and emotions, two terms we often use interchangeably. We need to be able to distinguish and label our thoughts and feelings as they help us become aware of them and understand them better.

The table below enumerates a few examples of thoughts and emotions.

Thoughts	*Emotions*
I completed my work in time.	I feel happy.
I have no friends.	I feel sad.
My spouse forgot my birthday.	I feel disappointed.
I had to do overtime.	I feel frustrated.
I passed my driving test.	I feel excited.
He should not take me for granted.	I feel angry.
I can never feel happy.	I feel hopeless.

CBT steps: The process of CBT can be divided into three basic steps:

  i. Identifying your automatic thoughts
  ii. Evaluating your automatic thoughts
  iii. Adapting a healthier or helpful thinking style

Identifying automatic thoughts

Humans spend every waking minute of the day thinking. In fact, our mind is active even while sleeping. On an average, the human mind has about 60,000–80,000 thoughts per day. Most of these thoughts are automatic; that is, they just pop up spontaneously in your mind. You are not even aware of them at a conscious level. Imagine what a task it would it be to keep a track of each one of them! Whenever you notice a shift in your emotional state or when you feel upset, angry or sad, focus on the thoughts that go through your mind. Make a note of these thoughts either immediately or at the end of the day. A simple three-column record sheet with columns for the situation, thoughts and feelings can help you identify the thoughts that are associated with a negative emotional state.

These questions can help you identify your thoughts:

- What was I thinking?
- What was going through my mind?
- What was I imagining?
- What was I expecting would happen?

Evaluating your automatic thoughts

The next step involves evaluating your automatic thoughts, which means looking objectively at your thought and determining if it is true, factual and realistic. We may realize on evaluation that even though our perception might be true, it might not be completely or absolutely true. You need to determine its usefulness or how helpful your current pattern of thinking is even if it is true.

These questions can help you evaluate your thoughts:

- What is the evidence for or against my thought?
- How true is it?
- What else could this situation mean?
- What would I advise my friend if they were in a similar situation?
- How will I feel about this five years from now?

Adapting a healthier thinking style

The next step involves adapting a more balanced, realistic and helpful way of thinking about the same situation. Adapting a healthier perspective will result in developing a more balanced emotional and behavioural response to various life situations.

These questions can help you find an alternative healthier way of thinking:

- What is another way to look at it?
- What can I do that will help me solve the problem?
- Is there something I can learn from this situation to help me do better next time?

One aspect of CBT involves self-reliance training, diversion methods and thought-stopping methods like the rubber band method explained earlier.

To summarize, our thoughts, behaviour and emotions are interlinked. It's impossible to think of good things and feel sad, right? If we are happy, our thoughts are good as well and we feel motivated and energetic. Also, it's impossible to feel relaxed when you are tense in the mind, and if your body is relaxed, it influences your mind too. So working on patient's negative thoughts (cognitions) and behaviours is the basis for CBT.

Other psychotherapies which can be used as per the patient's profile and therapist's expertise are:

Interpersonal psychotherapy: This method is used when interpersonal problems in a relationship are thought to be the main issues causing depression or worsening it. It addresses interpersonal relationships and is a highly selective therapy focusing on only one or two interpersonal problems at a time.

Psychoanalytic psychotherapy: It aims to change the patient's personality structure and not just reduce their symptoms of depression. Therapy is often offered for a longer duration of some years and not everyone is a candidate. The patient needs to have good 'ego strength', meaning when we dig into some of the unpleasant details of their childhood, they should be able to handle the anxiety and negative feelings that these memories evoke.

Most of us use eclectic therapy while treating patients, which is basically a mixture of different therapies and has a good effect on symptoms of the patient.

With the modern Midas touch of psychopharmacology, the branch which deals with producing and studying psychiatric medicines, we have more than 10 classes of antidepressant drugs and more than 50 actual drugs suited for various patient profiles and their symptoms. The picture and treatment of depression is quite clear now. We can exactly identify the offending neurotransmitters and their interplay which cause different types of depression symptoms, and the treatment can then be directed to that.

In some severe, recurrent or bipolar cases of depression, more than one drug may be needed for an indefinite period of time. But often, a patient's quality of life is way better with medicines with no major effect on the body. So typically, the question that I ask my patients of bipolar depression or recurrent depression is: 'You know you lead a normal or almost normal life with medicines, which don't have any major side effects, and you also know you suffer without taking medicines. Now the choice is yours, whether to lead a normal life with medicines or to suffer from depression with a poor quality of life without medicines.' Most of the people opt for medicines if we properly explain the rationale.

Hospitalization is often needed for patients with suicidal ideas, and electroconvulsive treatment may be considered for quicker relief. This topic is discussed further in the chapter on suicidality.

Effect of antidepressants

A little patience is required while taking treatment for any psychiatric disorder—our medicines don't act like the ones given for fever or vomiting which give relief in a single dose. It takes time to get better.

In the case of uncomplicated depression, a significant change in mood and overall reduction of symptoms are expected to happen in the initial two weeks after the first episode. However, to get total relief, six to eight weeks' treatment may be required.

In spite of getting total relief in symptoms, patients should not stop the medicines for at least four to six months (again, this is a general guideline and may differ from case to case). Later the medicines are tapered off. Just as we remove supports from new constructions little by little, antidepressants do a lot of chemical work at the level of brain receptors and need to be gradually reduced to prevent a relapse.

The side effect profile for most antidepressants is gentle, and they disappear with time.

Our medical science is inexact science. There are broad predictable things, but predicting exactly how much time a person will take to feel better or how much medicine is enough to guarantee recovery, is difficult. This is true for all other branches of medicine, too. Therefore, both the doctor and the patient need to be slightly flexible about the timeline and the dosage. One thing for sure is that all psychiatrists know the upper and lower limit for dosage and timelines for their action, and hence take care of these issues pretty well. What is communicated to patients is a statistical figure: most patients get better in these many days with this much dosage, but there could be individual differences.

Antidepressants not only uplift the mood and reduce anxiety, but they also act on rejection sensitivity (meaning when someone's benign or simple comment also affects the patient badly and they find it difficult to forget), preoccupation with the same thoughts (the same negative train of thought running repeatedly through the mind is also a common problem) and impulsivity (control over impulses of anger or of crying), reducing the severity of all of these and improving the overall feeling of well-being.

In addition to these effects, we have a variety of antidepressants that reduce the perception of physical pain and stop vomiting and acidity. Some antidepressants promote sleep, while others reduce lethargy and can have an awakening effect.

In severe cases or cases where bipolarity is suspected or a patient hears voices not audible to others, in addition to antidepressants, mood stabilizers or antipsychotics may be required for some duration.

When you are considering psychotherapy exclusively (as advised by your doctor or as per your insistence), these points should be kept in mind. One may have to expect a window of eight–10 weeks before seeing considerable improvement. Several factors come into play—whether the patient is taking active interest in the treatment, factors from the therapist such as countertransference issues and their rapport with each other, etc.

Other modalities of treatment

Electroconvulsive therapy

Electroconvulsive therapy or ECT (popularly called shock treatment) is one of the most effective, safest and fastest-acting treatments for resistant or severe depression with suicidal ideas.

Most movies show this as a cruel and inhuman procedure, where a violent patient is forcibly pushed down on the bed by attenders, a cotton pad is shoved into their mouth, electrodes are placed on either side of their scalp and current is passed. The patient's body starts convulsing and he is shown to become powerless post convulsion. Only a part of this picture is correct when it comes to administering ECTs in today's time.

ECT indeed works very well for violent patients, but it works well for depression and for certain other conditions too. Nowadays, direct ECT, which is without anaesthesia as shown in movies, is obsolete, and we use indirect ECT. A very short-acting general anaesthesia is administered, and the patient is made medically unconscious. The ECT is then administered carefully. We also regulate the amount of current passed and count the duration for which a patient should have convulsions for proper relief. Also, a prior consent for the procedure is taken from the patient or a relative, and it's not forced in cases of depression.

The side effects of ECTs, such as headache and temporary confusion, are often very gentle and self-limiting. And the procedure does not hurt the brain structures in any way. In fact, it improves the functioning of the brain through better communication between brain cells and higher levels of neurotransmitters. What do you do if your personal computer hangs? You restart the system, right? ECT works in a similar fashion and should undoubtedly be considered if recommended.

RTMS

Repetitive transcranial magnetic stimulation (RTMS) is a relatively new and emerging treatment for a variety of mental illnesses such as depression, OCD and addictions. During the procedure, a magnetic coil is placed across the head of the patient on the scalp and electromagnetic impulses are used here instead of an electric current, as used in ECT. The positioning of the coil is such that it targets only the specific areas of the brain which are responsible for the condition and doesn't affect other areas. This is an OPD procedure, and the patient doesn't require any anaesthesia. Most patients notice very mild side effects such as a crawling sensation in the scalp or a mild headache.

Vagal nerve stimulation

In this treatment, a small electronic device is implanted in the skin, something similar to pacemakers used for treating heart arrhythmia. The left vagus nerve is stimulated by this device for a specific period every day. This is useful for chronic and recurrent depression.

Phototherapy

This is typically useful for the seasonal affective disorder variant of depression, which typically happens in polar countries during winters due to less exposure to sunlight, leading to low moods. It is also useful for some sleep disorders particularly linked with jet lag or due to shift-duty sleep issues.

Ketamine

Ketamine belongs to the hallucinogen class of drugs and has been used for a long time as anaesthetic agent due to its property of dissociative anaesthesia, where a person feels dissociated from the environment, may get certain unreal experiences and experience a sense of euphoria. That's why this was also used in club parties with the name 'Vitamin k' or 'super k'. The medicinal use in psychiatry became popular in the last few years in the form of ketamine intravenous infusion. It's found to be very useful in patients with severe depression and suicidal tendencies.

When a family member is depressed

Now coming to the typical question that relatives or caregivers ask: what can we do to make the patient feel better? Avoid unhealthy attitudes towards the relative's illness, for example:

- **Guilt**: Feeling guilty for the patient's suffering. This is commonly seen in parents when their children suffer from depression. Guilt doesn't change anything constructively, and depression is multifactorial, so blaming yourself for a relative's depression is not justified.
- **Over-involvement**: Excessive involvement in the patient. Many relatives accompany the patient round the clock out of concern. Unless asked by a psychiatrist or if the patient is suicidal, this should be avoided. Everyone needs their space, and the patient may feel pressured if someone constantly accompanies them.
- **Criticism**: Criticizing the patient for their depression. People who don't understand the concept of depression sometimes do this. They hold the person's failures or their inability to cope with stressors responsible for depression and accuse the patient for it. This is not helpful, as the patient is really not responsible for whatever has happened, and it's definitely not a matter of choice.
- **Hostility**: Possibly destructive behaviour towards the patient's recovery from depression, such as discouraging them from taking medicines.
- **Indifference**: Staying aloof or unconcerned often worsens the feelings of depression for the patient. The majority of patients already feel unloved and lonely, so this attitude is in fact detrimental to recovery. Update your own knowledge about the illness, so you become less judgemental, can

understand the situation and the patient's symptoms and can offer effective help.

Understand that when a person says they feel lonely, it's the depression making them feel that way and you are probably not at fault. A person with depression often feels they have reached a point where nobody understands them; again, it's the depression causing this thought. After coming out of depression, the person may not feel like this, so don't take things personally when they say they are lonely or shout and become irritated at trivial reasons.

- Be a good listener and say this often: 'I am always willing to listen to you. Even though I may not have the solutions to fix your problems instantly, we can figure out a plan together for you.'
- Instead of asking the patient to go for a jog in the park or to exercise, engage in the activity together, like going for a walk together. If the person is exercising in the gym, ask if you can sit there with them. You can read quietly or listen to music if you don't work out. Often, patients report that someone being around them is reassuring and keeps their anxiety levels in check.
- You know what your relative likes, so making a list of the things they like and purposefully doing one or two of these every day can be helpful.
- Ensure there is adequate sunlight in all the rooms and let fresh air in the house. Children, plants and pets bring a lot of positivity and good energy.
- Acknowledge, appreciate and encourage each and every step your relative is taking to combat depression.
- Ensure they are taking their medicines and attending therapy sessions regularly. If the patient refuses to do

so, ask why and discuss your concerns with the treating doctor and therapist to find a way out.
- Talk to the treating psychiatrist with the patient's consent and ask about the possible ways in which you can help the patient, if any dysfunctional relationships are causing stress or if you or anyone else needs family therapy or family counselling.
- Give little responsibilities and daily chores to your relative once they start getting better, such as watering plants and buying vegetables from the nearby market. This helps distract them and restore a sense of self-esteem.
- Observe the patient when they are alone. Silently watching their activities can give you a sense of their current mental state—see if they are self-occupied, if they are appreciating something in the vicinity or if they are laughing at a funny show. Make a note of that and follow the trend in behaviour. Talk to the psychiatrist if needed.
- Do some daily or weekly activities together. Have one meal with the whole family sitting together or one outing in a week together.
- It's true that sometimes a hug is worth more than a thousand words. Touch is therapeutic. Practise hugging often, holding hands and cuddling—all these release oxytocin, a positive and bonding happy hormone, which helps in recovery. Touch communicates trust, love and the assurance that you are there with the patient in their battle against depression.
- Watch for suicidal gestures or significant changes which warrant medical attention (details in the chapter on suicidality).

When your friend is depressed

In addition to the points discussed above, learn to empathize, but maintain boundaries.

Empathy without boundaries is self-destruction. Honour your own limitations and ask for a break when required.

Here comes one important distinction between healthy and unhealthy emotions towards the patient. Understanding the difference between sympathy, empathy and compassion is very important. Sympathy is feeling bad for the patient, and it's not an entirely suitable emotion for the situation. Empathy is putting yourself in the patient's shoes—but learn to establish boundaries. Compassion is the feeling of warmth and showing care to help the patient get better.

Anxiety and depression bring negative vibes to relatives, dear ones and caretakers. It's important that they give priority to their self-care routines and, if required, ask for help from the mental healthcare provider if they feel overwhelmed.

Depression at work

We spend the maximum productive time with our colleagues at the workplace. We can thus easily sense the changes in their behaviour, performance and attitude. Colleagues can also support each other in times of temporary limitations, such as when a smaller workload is necessary or more flexibility is required when a person is recovering from depression. Colleagues can also be more accountable for changes in the lifestyle of patients such as a healthier diet, exercise and reduction in smoking and consumption of alcohol.

What should managers or the leadership do? Managers are the gatekeepers for many things—they know if the work conditions are conducive to performance and job satisfaction, and can thus alter them accordingly to a certain extent. They know their people well and can identify the at-risk population and also understand if the workload on some individual is unfair. They can ensure that various organizational changes are communicated well with appropriate impact.

So managers can act as stress inducers, stress identifiers and even stress busters. In addition to having an employee assistance programme and a proper referral system for further management, managers can follow this model we call RESPECT:

R: regular contact
E and **S**: empathetic and supportive communication
P: practical help and not any kind of psychotherapy
E: encouraging help seeking
C: considering return to work
T: telling employees that the door is open for the next level of help

Often a supportive work environment can reduce absenteeism due to mental illness, and improve productivity and retention of employees in the long run.

These are supportive factors and cannot take the mainstay of the treatment of depression. Depression has to be treated by a qualified mental healthcare provider.

After depression

Here are some observations from patients who have overcome depression:

- **More enjoyment in simple things**: I remember sitting with a patient in a session who was on maintenance treatment for depression. I cracked a silly joke and we had a hearty laugh (by the way, we often try to see if the patient has mood reactivity in spite of having depression by cracking a joke; if they are able to smile or laugh at our joke, it's a sign that they still possess or are gaining mood reactivity). What was really satisfying was my patient's comment, 'Doctor, you know I am laughing this much after years. I had lost that ability and I know I am getting it back.'

So patients start enjoying little things more when they come out of depression. Most of them say that depression has made them aware of simple and beautiful things in life and they appreciate them more often.

- **More empathy and more compassion**: As they say, be in their shoes to understand what goes on in their life. Many patients who come out of depression look at society and its problems—both obvious and subtle problems/issues—with more empathy and are more helpful.
- **A less judgmental attitude**: I remember one of my patients telling me, 'Doctor, I used to get irritated with a mentally challenged child who used to throw stones at my house every night. I was in fact thinking of teaching him a lesson. Now that I have come out of depression, I have a better understanding of mental health and what it entails. I don't judge him now. I know he doesn't know what he is doing. I have even learned to give the benefit of the doubt to people at home and in my office when they are going through a stressful situation.'

Once out of depression, most people become more flexible, less irritable and less judgemental about themselves and others.
- **Educators in the field of mental health**: In my practice, almost 20 per cent of the patients come to us via reference

of other patients. When these recovered patients share their success stories, see the difference in themselves and educate others about the invisible illness they went through, people trust them all the more. I am thankful to all the celebrities like Deepika Padukone, Ileana D'Cruz, Anushka Sharma and Varun Dhawan for sharing their stories about depression and anxiety, for putting in efforts for greater awareness and education about mental health and for destigmatization of its treatment. They have a big impact value, which they are using for the right purpose.

Even corporates have been a big game changer. Through their inclusivity and diversity policy, people are becoming more aware about their mental health illnesses. In fact, in some corporates, where I work as a trainer, we celebrate happy mind days (like cancer survivors' day), where we invite people to talk about their journeys.

Obviously, awareness by these methods is increasing in metros, but rural areas still have very little awareness about mental health.

- **Self-awareness, self-love and care**: After going through dark times alone—full of self-doubt, inappropriate guilt and self-hatred—most patients learn about the importance of self-acceptance, the awareness of emotions, how to take care of and love oneself unconditionally. They learn to keep some time aside in the day to reflect upon their life and self. After all, every dark cloud has a silver lining.

7
I WANT TO LIVE

We are all born with the capacity to take our own life. Every year, millions of people exercise this option—some succeed, some don't. Suicides have been occurring for ages. In the Ramayana and the Mahabharata, we see several references to suicide. In the Ramayana, after Lord Rama dropped his mortal frame, many people in Ayodhya died by suicide by drowning in the river Sharayu due to overwhelming sadness. Rishi Dadhichi sacrificed his life to help the gods in war. The gods used his bones, which had special powers, to make a *vajra* (weapon) and used it to kill the asuras (demons). Sati, a former practice in India whereby a wife would throw herself on to her husband's funeral pyre, is another form of suicide. Suicide bombers too fall in this category.

Mahasamadhi taken by yogis also comes under the umbrella of suicide, although it's a socially sanctioned form. This is different because although the intent is to die, they don't use any external measures to kill themselves. They exit their prana through Brahmarandhra using their yogic power. The same applies to Prayopaveshana, a method of chronic suicide which is socially sanctioned as well, where a person gradually and systematically reduces their food intake to survive only on water and then only on air. It's gradual death without using any external means.

There are other forms of slow suicides as well. For example, a person suffering from chronic kidney failure is prescribed dialysis but does not go for it regularly or if a diabetic doesn't take their medicines or adopt lifestyle measures to control it. This amounts to self-harm, as they are cutting their own life short by not taking the treatment when it's necessary.

No religion justifies suicide. As per Hinduism, the departed soul remains stuck in darkness for long period of time after suicide.[43] Dropping your body before the actual time is not justified in spirituality. When the time comes, our consent is not taken. Our current life is created by the Supreme Power with the consent of our soul for gaining more maturity. Before we came here, the syllabus for our life was decided, a syllabus which is unique for each one of us. How can we leave before completing that? For example, can we enter the eleventh standard without clearing the tenth? If we leave the exam midway, we have to come back and finish it the next time—there is no excuse from it. The same logic is applicable to suicide.[44] These circumstances and experiences are created to teach us something. We need to master them and there is no escape midway. Hence, suicide is never the answer.

An attempted suicide is a crime as per Section 309 of the Indian Penal Code. Even though the IPC section continues to exist, in March 2017, the Indian parliament passed the Mental Healthcare Act 2017 that tries to decriminalize attempted suicide and makes a presumption of severe stress in case of attempt to commit suicide (Section 115).[45]

---

[43] V., Jayaram., 'About suicides in Hinduism', *Hinduweb.com*, https://bit.ly/3N3lRmW. Accessed on 21 March 2022.
[44] Ibid.
[45] 'Mental health bill decriminalising suicide passed by Parliament', *The Indian Express*, 27 March 2017, https://bit.ly/3oYwBIJ. Accessed on 18 February 2022.

Any suicide becomes a topic of discussion in society. In the families where a member dies by suicide, the relatives go through immense pain, unanswered questions and a near lifetime of regret for not being able to gauge the suicidal thoughts and tendencies of the loved one. Sometimes they suffer from guilt as well, called 'survivor's guilt'. As is very aptly said, suicide never takes away the pain, it simply gives it to someone else.

When we hear and read so many negative things about suicides, why do so many suicides continue to happen? This is because the people who take this path feel that there is no way left for them other than ending their life. For them, life hurts a lot more than death. As per a number of surveys and studies, more than 80 per cent of the people who attempt or die by suicide suffer from depression.[46] Because of depression, inappropriate guilt, a feeling that they are a failure, and hopelessness worsen. If not interrupted, this train of thoughts can become suicidal. Hence, depression must be treated well in time. There are other reasons for attempting or choosing death by suicide as well, and we will look at them later in the chapter.

Demographics of suicide

Let's understand the prevalence of suicide. As per WHO data, close to 800,000 people die by suicide every year. Out of these, 1,35,000 (17 per cent) are residents of India.[47] There are indications that for each adult who dies by suicide, there may be

---

[46] Shahtahmasebi, Said, 'Examining the Claim that 80–90% of Suicide Cases Had Depression', *Front Public Health*, 2013; 1: 62, https://bit.ly/3KCn0QJ. Accessed on 12 April 2022.

[47] 'Accidental Deaths & Suicides in India – 2019', National Crime Records Bureau, Updated on 20 January 2022, https://bit.ly/3wnhwVL. Accessed on 21 March 2022.

more than 20 others attempting. This translates to one person dying by suicide every 40 seconds, and one person attempting suicide every 3 seconds. Generally, more women attempt suicide than men, but success rate of men is higher than women's.[48] The most prevalent age group that attempts or dies by suicide is between 15 and 45. Young people attempt or die by suicide more due to various pressures that they are unable to cope with. Nowadays, the prevalence of suicide has increased in children as well. In the elderly population, although the overall prevalence of suicide is lower, their rate of success is high. Hanging followed by poisoning are the most common methods of dying by suicide in India.[49] Overall, the prevalence of suicide is much higher in cities, although in the last few years, several farmers' suicides have been reported, predominantly in rural parts of India. The unmarried population and people living alone also attempt suicide more frequently. Marriage and children are considered major protective factors. Low levels of education and unemployment are also risk factors for depression and suicide.

Types of suicides

What are the types of suicide? Broadly speaking, as per French sociologist Émile Durkheim, there are four types of suicides. These types are named on the basis of the reasons for dying by suicides.

---

[48]Tsirigotis, Konstantinos et al., 'Gender differentiation in methods of suicide attempts', *Medical Science Monitor*, 2011, 17(8): PH65–PH70, https://bit.ly/377Q6sW. Accessed on 12 April 2022.

[49]Rane, Anil and Abhijit Nadkarni, 'Suicide in India: a systematic review', *Shanghai Archives of Psychiatry*, April 2014; 26(2): 69–80, https://bit.ly/3udE1dd. Accessed on 21 March 2022.

Egoistic suicide: The most common type of suicide, it is characterized by high isolation. The person is very loosely integrated into society and find themselves failing to meet societal expectations. Let's look at one example.

The sister of one of my patients had died by suicide. She was an introvert and preferred being alone, without significant friendships from early childhood. She used to spend most of her days watching TV and reading books. She could never stick to one job due to a lack of minimal social skills and was unmarried. When her sister asked her about her future plans, she seemed lost and aimless. Although her life was full of anxiety and darkness, she never expressed her thoughts to anyone. When I was dealing with the sister's survivor's guilt, I sensed that her suicide was egoistic.

Previously, when alternate orientations were less socially acceptable, some people from the LGBTQ community would attempt or die by suicide as they saw themselves as misfits in the community and were either bullied, made fun of or socially disrespected. Unable to integrate, they would die by suicide.[50]

Altruistic suicide: In this type of suicide, contrary to egoistic suicide, excessive social integration in a group is the problem. Altruism means a social behaviour of doing good for the benefit of community.

When a person sacrifices their life to save other members of the society, for the benefit of a group or for the purpose of preserving tradition, it's termed 'altruistic suicide' or 'benevolent suicide'. The individual feels obliged to perform a self-destructive act as a result of an obligation to society. Also, their self-destructive act is appreciated by that class of society. Here, the

---

[50] Kleitsch, David, *Community in a Virtual Environment: Can YouTube Build Community for LGBT Youth?* Appalachian State University, 2015.

person dying by suicide has no sense of self outside that societal circle. Hence, the idea of that circle becomes life for that person, which they may sacrifice for the betterment of society.

An example of this type of suicide is suicide bombers. When an individual becomes a suicide bomber, their act is respected and valued by a group or class of society, whose beliefs have become most important to that individual. In the practice of sati, the woman was considered pious and pure if she jumped into her husband's funeral pyre.

I remember seeing a depressed adolescent in my clinic, whose mother had died by suicide a few months back. When I went through the details of the case, I found that she had been diagnosed with advanced-stage cancer. It was a very time-consuming and stressful period for the family members and treatment expenses were so high that the family had to sell off one of their assets. This pressure was taking a toll on her mind, and one day, she consumed all the painkillers and sleeping pills she had and died by suicide. Her suicide note cited that everyone would be better off without her. This was also a type of altruistic suicide done in the larger interest of the family as perceived by the patient.

Anomic suicide: Anomic suicides occur when a person's integration with the community is suddenly disturbed and they die by suicide due to extreme stress. This typically happens, for example, when a person suffers from a sudden and drastic financial loss. When a person feels that, due to a sudden change in their circumstances beyond their control, life is not going to be the same, it triggers an unbearable panic reaction, which may eventually result in suicide. We have seen people attempting or dying by suicide with major changes in the share market. I have also seen such suicides taking place when some secrets were revealed and the patient found it difficult to cope with their new reality.

This reminds me of an adolescent patient I had examined in the emergency department after an attempted hanging. Luckily, the fan was loosely attached to the ceiling, and hence this person fell down on the bed along with the rope and the fan. When I interviewed him, he said he was really happy with his family, which comprised his parents and him. However, one day, he returned home early from work to find his mother getting intimate with one of his father's friends. He felt betrayed by his own mother and experienced tremendous stress thereafter. He started questioning family values and could not share this situation with anyone. This sudden shift resulted in a suicide attempt the next day.

Fatalistic suicide: When a suicide happens in a very strictly regulated environment, where a person feels escape from that environment is impossible, then it is defined as fatalistic suicide. Suicides occurring in prisons or by women who are unable to conceive and are subjected to constant societal pressures fall in this category.

I remember seeing a young, beautiful woman in my clinic a few years back. She had come with her parents to see me. When I interviewed her privately, she told me that the depression was because her family refused to accept her relationship with a man. The couple desperately wanted to get married, but her parents threatened her that if she continued to see that man, both of them would die by suicide. This woman showed all symptoms of depression, and I prescribed medications and advised family counselling. The family agreed to come for counselling after a few days, but they never turned up. After a few months, her mother came to see me and gave me the news that their daughter had died by suicide almost a month back. Before ending her life, she had sent out a message to all her WhatsApp groups saying, 'It's impossible to live without my boyfriend and my family won't allow me to marry him at any cost, hence I feel tormented by pressure from my family and really cannot live like this.'

Copycat suicide or imitation suicide: When a celebrity suicide happens, we see another type of suicide called copycat suicide or imitation suicide. As the name suggests, it's basically copying somebody else's behaviour. People may also attempt it when someone close to them dies by suicide. A person might be feeling low, contemplating suicide or going through situations similar to the celebrity who had died by suicide (as portrayed by the media). They may then feel that this is the answer to their problems as well and may get motivated to do the same.

One of my patients who attempted suicide immediately after a celebrity died by suicide told me, 'I thought it's easier to consider suicide as the solution as I was and I still am very impressed and influenced by that actor. If that celebrity had not done it, I probably would not have considered it in my weak moments. I thought when a person whom I am following and idolizing finds relief in suicide, it could be a solution to my problems too.'

In copycat suicides, the media plays an important role. Often, it's just not plain news but the views of related and unrelated people and the glorification and sensationalization of the suicide that is counterproductive. We will discuss the guidelines the media and other people should follow to reduce these counterproductive effects in the later part of this chapter.

Suicide pact: As the name suggests, a suicide pact is an agreement in which two or more people decide to kill themselves simultaneously. This is a fairly uncommon mode of suicide. Usually, both parties know each other, and the majority of the times they are husband and wife. One of them has a major psychiatric disorder, or one is very dominating and the other is submissive and may not have much voice in the relationship.

Reasons and risk factors

When we try to understand the reasons, triggers and risk factors associated with suicide, several things remain unclear. As in the cases of completed suicides this is always a retrospective study, it's called 'psychological autopsy', which involves going through available records, and interviewing relatives and mental healthcare providers, if they were involved. All these are attempts to understand what had gone wrong. This method has limitations, as it's the collected data that may not always be perfect and clear. Nevertheless, it has helped understand the dynamics of suicide to a great extent and also in identifying risk factors and prevention and precautionary measures.

Let's understand suicide dynamics through some famous movies, as they often show the psychology of affected individuals very well. Such representations appeal to the masses and can be a medium for studying various aspects of life if accurately shown.

Let's look at *Aitraaz*. Sonia Roy (Priyanka Chopra) files a case against Raj Malhotra (Akshay Kumar) for sexual harassment. Her case seems very strong in the beginning. As the movie progresses, it takes interesting twists and turns and finally Sonia is exposed for her ambitions and destructive nature. Unable to accept the criticism she faces and such a fall in social status, she dies by suicide. As the film depicts, the reason for the suicide is the sudden downward change in social or economic status, where you find coping is impossible.

Another excellent movie, *3 Idiots*, shows three suicide attempts—two people succeed and one fails. The first case is a student at the prestigious institution who hangs himself after failing to complete his science experiment in time. The second case is the son of the dean, who jumps in front of a train due to the family pressure of pursuing a career in which he is not interested. The third case shown is one of the main characters, Raju Rastogi, played by Sharman Joshi, who attempts suicide when he feels he cannot choose between two equally painful situations: revealing the names of his co-conspirators (his best friends) for a prank done on the dean or getting expelled from college. Feeling helpless, he chooses to jump off a building.

In *Chhichhore*, academic failure or failure to secure admission in a prestigious institute becomes a question of life and death for a teenager, who attempts to take his own life.

In *Mohabbatein*, Megha Shankar (Aishwarya Rai) comes to know that her father (Amitabh Bachchan) had sabotaged the career of the man she loves (played by Shah Rukh Khan), removed him from school and would never approve of her relationship with him. She dies by suicide in frustration.

In the movie *Fiza*, when a mother learns that her son has become a terrorist, she feels that she is a failure as a mother and drowns herself in the sea.

In the movie *Padmaavat*, Rani Padmavati and several other women jump into the fire and perform jauhar to protect their pride when the Mughals try to capture them after killing their king and other soldiers of the kingdom.

In *Karthik Calling Karthik*, the male lead is shown to have schizophrenia and tries to attempt suicide twice, once due to stress at work and again when he is fed up of hearing voices in his head and feels there is no escape.

In *Anjaana Anjaani*, two depressed people decide to help each other die by suicide by signing a pact.

In *Kaabil*, after being raped by local influential people,

Supriya Sharma (Yami Gautam) takes her life due to shame and sadness.

In all these stories, although the triggers are different, the common thread is unbearable pain, intolerable frustration and the inability to see any way out except taking one's own life.

The role of depression

As stated earlier, almost 80 per cent of the people who attempt suicide suffer from some kind of mental illness. Out of these people, four-fifths suffer from depression, which significantly affects our thinking patterns and paralyses rational thinking when it becomes severe, giving rise to a lot of irrational and inappropriate thought patterns.

In all these cases, the most important factor is the feeling of hopelessness—an event or a situation makes the person so hopeless about the future that they feel hopeless about the self, family, society and God, and sometimes feel helplessness too. They may feel that escape from such a situation is impossible, but neither are they able to live with it. A suicidal person may feel they are totally worthless and of no use to their family, society or to anybody else. Thus, hopelessness, helplessness and worthlessness are the most important feelings that compel a person to die by suicide. Asking about these three things is of paramount importance in our clinical interview. Among the three, the most important is hopelessness. As concluded in different studies, it's a very strong indicator that a person may attempt suicide.[51]

---

[51] Klonsky, David E. et al., 'Hopelessness as a predictor of attempted suicide among first admission patients with psychosis: A 10-year cohort study', *Suicide and Life-Threatening Behaviour*, 2012 February; 42(1): 1–10, https://bit.

Antidepressants

A point to be noted is that antidepressants in earlier weeks of treatment are known to increase suicidal behaviour, particularly in young and severely depressed patients. This is called 'paradoxical suicide'. In severely depressed patients, antidepressants may improve their psychomotor activities even before the mood is uplifted, causing the patient, who was feeling slothful and lethargic earlier, motivated to carry out routine activities and consequently act on desires for self-harm. After a few weeks, once the mood lifts and thoughts become more positive, this risk reduces.

Schizophrenia

Other than depression, psychiatric illnesses like schizophrenia, where a patient repeatedly hears voices inaudible to others, commanding them to self-harm, may lead to suicide. Listening to the same kind of commands repeatedly may direct the mind to do the act.

I remember a case of this kind from my residency days. There was an emergency call from the casualty ward. A male patient had chopped off his private organ, leading to a lot of blood loss. A minor surgery had to be done by the urologist to relieve urinary retention. The patient was still very aggressive, muttering to himself. I gave him medications to calm him down. I was sitting in the next room, observing him quietly. After two hours, he said he wanted to wash his face and do some gargling to freshen up. I asked a ward boy to accompany him to the

---

ly/3L37T2q. Accessed on 21 March 2022; Beck, Aaron T. et al., 'Hopelessness and Suicidal Behavior: An Overview', *JAMA Network*, 15 December 1975, https://bit.ly/3CVLKAm. Accessed on 21 March 2022.

washroom and keep a close watch on him. After washing his face, he suddenly broke the glass window near the wash basin and sustained a major injury on three of his fingers. After getting treated by several specialities in the ICU, he was finally shifted to our psychiatry ward and given ECTs and medicines, which helped him recover. At the time, his wife and very young child were quietly waiting outside our wards. When it was time to discharge him, I didn't ask him any of the routine questions, like if he was hearing voices or if he was suspicious of someone. Instead, I just asked him, 'You will stay well, right?' Hearing this question, he started crying uncontrollably.

'Doctor, I was unable to decide…understand…what was right and what was wrong. Constant voices in my ears were commanding, "Cut, cut the penis…cut the fingers". I got so overwhelmed that I followed those commands, and look what irreversible damage I have done.' In the whole process, his wife was sobbing silently in the corner, holding on to her child tightly.

Commanding hallucinations are a well-known risk factor for suicide attempts in schizophrenia, and surprisingly, the content of these hallucinations is common across all cultures—sexually derogatory content, such as ordering patients to mutilate their private organs, shave their eyebrows and then attempting suicide.

After the patient recovers from psychosis (meaning a kind of madness), they are still at risk of attempting suicide as they are in the know of what they have lost in life. I remember one of my patients telling me how schizophrenia has stolen his mind and his life, too. In this phase, close observation from psychiatrists is required, with a probable use of antidepressants.

Anxiety disorders

In anxiety disorders, sometimes a person loses balance and attempts suicide. Sometimes during a bout of anxiety, with palpitations, choking sensations and cold hands and feet, the mind gets so restless and loses control that the person may use some extreme ways to get rid of the anxiety, such as jumping off a building. In fact, people who have survived suicide attempts resulting from panic anxiety often say that anxiety makes the mind so powerless that they end up attempting something which they are actually scared of. They are definitely scared of dying, but they lose control and take such steps out of fear and anxiety.

Drug abuse and suicidality

As per various studies, using any substance—nicotine, alcohol, cannabis or opioids—increases the risk of suicide sixfold.[52] Patients may also use substances which they are addicted to as a means for attempting suicide.

When associated with depression, alcohol addiction further increases the risk of suicide. Alcohol may directly influence judgement and decision-making capacity, reduce inhibitions and increase impulsivity, aggression and self-harm tendencies. Also, although alcohol gives temporary relief from stress and the patient may find some respite by consuming it, it worsens the depression in the long term, as it is a central nervous system depressant. It also increases the tendency to harm the self and others.

Opioid addicts, such as brown sugar addicts, have some

---

[52] Dragisic, Tatjana et al., 'Drug Addiction as Risk for Suicide Attempts', *Materia Socio Medica*, 8 June 2015, https://bit.ly/3N9mWK7. Accessed on 21 March 2022; 'Suicide and Substance Abuse', *Addiction Center*, https://bit.ly/3L1MDuc. Accessed on 21 March 2022.

additional issues. In addition to mood and personality changes due to the consumption of brown sugar, they may run out of money as opioids are very expensive and are difficult to procure (it's illegal to sell or use them without medical indications). One may have to steal money, stay away from family or suffer multiple infections, all of which compound the stress further.

Also, relationship issues, job losses, helplessness over the addiction and relapses increase suicidal tendencies.

Chronic pain and illnesses

Chronic debilitating illnesses, terminal diseases, disfiguring illnesses and illnesses in which daily activities become a challenge are risk factors for suicide. In such cases, instead of ending one's life, escaping from the pain is the primary motive.

When terminally ill cancer patients attempt suicide, it is the intolerable physical pain that compels them to take this extreme decision. If identified on time, adequate pain management and anxiolytics can be of immense help. It's not only physical pain in incurable diseases that makes them suicidal; in fact, it's what we call 'total pain' in psychiatry, which makes them more vulnerable to psychiatric issues. It comprises physical pain, psychological pain, social issues and spiritual conflict.

A person suffering from depression has a pain threshold that is substantially reduced. If physical pain occurs at this point, even pain that would normally be a 5/10 will be perceived as 10/10 because of the increased pain perception.

Psychological issues in incurable diseases may be because of anger over the disease, and depression and anxiety associated with the disease, its treatment and the future.

Social issues could be due to isolation and restrictions posed by the illness and its treatment. Often, it becomes difficult for a person to see relatives going about their routine work, planning their activities smoothly and still being able to enjoy life without involving them.

Spiritual pain could be due to the question 'Why me?' or anger at God, feeling hopeless about the situation, or thinking it's a punishment for some past bad deeds. So, a psychiatrist's job is to resolve these conflicts with counselling and proper medicines.

Genetic factors

The genetic factor is not a very strong cause for suicide, but there is a definite association between genetics and suicide. If one or more family members have died by suicide, then there is a two to three time higher risk of other members dying by suicide in the family. Multiple genes have been found responsible for suicidality, although the genetic component is just one factor in the multiple causality theory.[53]

A previous suicide attempt is a major indicator that another attempt may be made.

Planned or impulsive?

There are two kinds of suicide attempts: planned and impulsive. Impulsive attempts may not succeed in suicide completion, whereas in planned suicide, the attempter's suicide completion rates are very high. A plan indicates the severity of the intent.

Planned attempts

In this case, the thought of suicide has been ongoing in the patient's mind for a long time and they are most likely going

---

[53] Zai, Clement C. et al., 'Genetic Factors and Suicidal Behavior', in *The Neurobiological Basis of Suicide,* Yogesh Dwivedi (ed), Chapter 11, https://bit.ly/3LUvO4I. Accessed on 12 April 2022.

through psychiatric disorders. They plan the event well in advance as well as the means of the suicide. They may also give hints months or days prior to the attempt and put their affairs in order. A definite change in their behaviour may also occur. They may become more secretive and isolate themselves for some time. If a planned attempt fails, there is a very high risk that the attempter will try again, and hence, needs good treatment by a psychiatrist and also close monitoring.

Impulsive attempts

Such attempts are a result of sudden stress such as an argument or failure in an exam. As the name suggests, such attempts are impulsive and often without planning. They use whatever means are available to attempt suicide and may not have a major psychiatric disorder. They may also do it in front of people and may call others for help after attempting suicide.

There are patients with an unstable personality who attempt self-harm without having the intent to die. They do trivial injuries to themselves and in a repetitive manner. Such behaviour often causes distress to family members. It's a constant threat to them, as the affected person can potentially self-harm if under stress. Emotionally unstable personalities, such as people with borderline personality disorder, very often attempt suicide. These people are generally depressed since early adolescence, have anger dysregulation issues, and can sometimes have micropsychotic episodes, such as being very unpredictable and unreasonable at times and being normal the next morning. Their relationships can be very intense but short-lived. They are self-absorbed and always have the feeling that they are victims of situations in life. Because of this constant pain and their impulsive nature, they very often attempt suicide. These are attempts intended to draw attention, which could be misunderstood by family and friends, so they may make fun of them, ignore them or get irritated with them.

While treating borderline personalities, we need to understand why there is a need to gain attention. It's often insecurity or mistrust about life which makes them vulnerable, and they do it again, and again. Also, by slashing their wrists or banging their head against the wall, a sudden gush of endorphins, which are natural mood lifters, is released in the brain. They gain the attention of others as well through such behaviour. When we treat them, in addition to psychotherapy and medicines which control these behaviours very well, we need to teach them better coping strategies and easy ways of releasing endorphins, such as good aerobic exercise, and better ways of catharsis such as scribbling on paper or kick-boxing a pillow.

Why don't patients reach out?

Listed below are some of the common reasons why suicidal patients do not reach out for help:

- There is a stigma associated with suicidality, and they feel others may be judgmental towards their thoughts and feelings.
- The majority of them are already suffering from depression and inappropriate guilt and may feel their family is burdened because of them. So, they don't want to be a burden by continuing to live.
- They fear that they may not be understood enough and, instead of getting support, empathy and compassion from others, they may get criticism. They fear that they will be called 'attention seeking', and people may not take them seriously or may make fun of them.

- They may not feel it's safe to talk about their feelings and thoughts to others, and others may take harsh steps such as putting them in psychiatric nursing homes.

How to identify if someone is suicidal?

Every suicide is a tragedy, a cry for help that was not answered in time. And we should be vigilant enough to recognize these signs or gestures given by a suicidal patient.

A single clue or gesture doesn't mean that the person is suicidal, but a cluster of such clues definitely needs timely attention from friends and relatives. A suicidal person often gives clues, and these could be expressed in different forms as follows:

- Giving away valuables and priced possessions
- Making a will
- Giving some terminal instructions
- Setting business matters in order
- Making phone calls and sending emails to friends and relatives saying goodbye
- Saying things like 'everyone in the family would be in a better place without me' or 'people would probably understand my importance when I am gone,' etc.
- Showing a sudden sense of happiness and freedom in a depressed patient, as he gets the answer to unresolved conflicts or pain
- Social isolation, or in other words, staying aloof even from family members. This happens as they feel nobody can understand their situation and the reason for social isolation, often indicating a so-called 'point of no return'[54]

---

[54] In suicidology, the point of no return is the last stage, where they cut ties with the outer world.

- Looking up ways to die by suicide on the Internet
- Writing poetry, snippets and stories related to death in their journals or social media profiles
- Most important, expressing suicidal ideas. We dismiss the issue if someone says they are feeling suicidal because we believe it's just empty words. But in reality, nearly 60–70 per cent people give hints before dying by suicide. So, we need to take it seriously if someone exhibits any such behaviour.

Dos and don'ts

Dos

Ask directly the following questions:

- Do you have a *plan*?
  (As stated earlier, a plan indicates the severity of suicidal intention and also shows that the patient is contemplating suicide for a long time, hence the distress is severe.)
- Do you have the *means* available to hurt yourself?
- *When* do you plan on hurting yourself?
- Have you *told* anyone about it?
- *How long* have you been thinking about suicide?
  (The available means, the fixed date, not telling anyone and contemplating suicide for a long time—these indicate that the person needs immediate help. See if you can help without a power struggle. If they confide in you the means, see if you can get rid of them. Keep all sharp and harmful objects away from the patient and keep a minimum quantity of medicines with them.)

- Do you really want to die, or do you want the pain to go away?
  (People often die by suicide as a result of unbearable stress from which they can't find a way out. The sense of being trapped in that situation makes them feel suicidal. If a solution is offered to that problem from a third person's perspective, they may reconsider the idea of suicide.)

Be a good listener: Sound calm and understanding. Use reflective listening. Ask questions that help define the problem and use language appropriate for the age of the person involved.

Show that you care: Be positive, emphasize more desirable alternatives and help them identify sources of support.

Get help: Find out people who are a part of or are willing to be a part of the patient's support system, such as family members, friends, a psychiatrist or co-workers. Involve them in taking care of the patient. There are suicide prevention helplines in all parts of India. Their contact details can be easily found on the Internet, and many of them function 24/7. Volunteers or employees working with them are experienced at counselling suicidal patients and helping them effectively till you can take them to a psychiatrist.

Provide physical contact: Physical contact in the form of holding hands, hugging if possible and appropriate touch signifies a lot when a patient is depressed. It gives them a sense of warmth and security.

Specifically ask about:

- **Psychological pain**: hurt, anguish, misery
- **Stress**: feeling pressured or overwhelmed

- **Agitation**: emotional urgency, the need to take action
- **Hopelessness**: the sense that things will never get better, no matter what
- **Self-hate**: disliking oneself; no self-esteem or self-respect. In such cases, the patient's anger is directed inwards.
- **Actions**: any steps taken towards implementing a plan, such as buying extra medicines or pesticide.
- **Intent**: what they hope to achieve by suicide or what suicide means to the patient. Is it to end physical pain? Or, financial troubles for the family?
- **Treatment for psychiatric issues involves asking**:
  - Do you have a therapist or doctor?
  - Are you seeing them even now?
  - Are you taking your medications?

In known cases of depression, there is the possibility of other psychiatric illnesses. The patient may have stopped their medicines and/or stopped seeing a doctor. Such actions can give relatives or friends a clue about their state of mind.

Don'ts

Don't sidestep the issue: Suicidal thoughts may be occupying the patient's whole world, and they need to be addressed. Ignoring them won't help them.

Don't sound shocked: This prevents the suicidal person from talking further with you.

Don't debate or argue with the person: This is not the right time to tell them how suicide is not the right solution to their problems or that their reasons don't justify suicide. This does more harm than good.

Don't overreact: Don't be shocked by anything they say. Listen patiently and express the willingness to help.

Don't rush: Establish contact and take the person to someone who can help; you are not trying to completely resolve the crisis.

Don't minimize the person's concerns: 'This is not worth killing yourself over.' Such a statement is not helpful to the patient. Instead, remember to acknowledge their issues by saying, 'I understand it's very upsetting for you. Let's figure out how you can be helped.'

Don't be overly analytical: Looking for hidden motivations, even if you succeed in bringing covered conflicts or motives to surface, will not help, as the person may react to such discussions very violently. You may share your concerns with the treating doctor.

Don't use reverse psychology: Don't encourage the patient to do what you don't actually want them to do. For example, don't say things like, 'Okay, you want to do it, show me, let me see.' The person may not understand your intentions and may end up actually attempting or dying by suicide in a fit of anger, assuming that you are challenging them, something which you don't want.

Don't say things like:

- 'It's just a phase.'
- 'You'll snap out of it.'
- 'Stop being so selfish.'
- 'You're just trying to get attention.'
- 'Get over it.'

Don't leave the patient alone: This is undoubtedly the most important point. Constant supervision is needed till you meet a psychiatrist. Supervised food and medications are required. Keep sharp and harmful objects away from the patient.

Don't feel responsible for saving the person: Remember, you are responsive but not responsible for saving that person. In spite of all your efforts, if the suicide still happens, don't hold yourself responsible for the person's death. There are many factors beyond anyone's control, and whatever you can do should be done.

What do psychiatrists do in such circumstances?

All psychiatrists advise hospital admission for suicidal patients, as there is no safe place like a hospital for us to keep a watch on the patient and treat them. Also, every suicidal patient must meet a psychiatrist, not a counsellor or psychologist. Counselling can neither reach the mind of a suicidal patient, nor can it address the severity of the clinical condition of 99 per cent of the suicidal patients. Medicines are prescribed for suicidality as per the underlying psychiatric disorder. We have excellent medicines to treat suicidal ideas. Also, electroconvulsive therapy (shock treatment) is extremely effective, safe and fast-acting when it comes to treating suicidal patients. If the treating psychiatrist recommends it, relatives should definitely consider it. Later, once the patient stabilizes, psychotherapy sessions can be conducted.

I would like to share an example from my residency days. I was in the second year of my MD programme. A middle-aged woman was admitted to our ward with suicidal tendencies. She had lost her teenaged son in an accident six months back and was in severe depression. For suicidal patients, we normally give the first bed in the ward, so that full attention can be given to them. We did the same for her, and slowly and steadily, she started responding to medical treatment and electroconvulsive therapies. I got along very well with her and her daughter, who was almost my age. We had a lot of common interests such as love for music, reading and writing. After a week, she told me during an evening therapy session, 'Although I lost my son, I can still do a lot in my life. I can dedicate some small work to his memory.' I was assured with that positive talk.

After a few days, the senior doctors evaluated her. Once they were satisfied, her date of discharge was finalized after a week. A day prior to her discharge she gifted small mirrors to every patient in the ward, indicating that this is real and not the world they feel or hear (this gift was very relevant for schizophrenia patients who get hallucinations and perceive the experiences which are not real, as ours was a tertiary care centre for schizophrenia). She gifted me a bunch of good books and CDs of some classical ragas with a thank you note. It was raining very heavily that night. Early in the morning, the landline in my hostel room rang. I was puzzled, as I was not on night duty. The staff nurse was on the line. She told me that the patient hanged herself in the morning. I froze. I felt as if I tried to pull somebody who was falling off a cliff, and at the last moment that person pushed me away. I was a student at the time, and I took a long time to learn the lesson that suicide dynamics are still not completely clear to anyone.

Each one of us, doctors or others, have our limitations. The human mind, with its complexities, is sometimes beyond our understanding. Does this mean we cannot help in preventing suicides? No, we can in many cases, and these examples are rare but help us understand our limitations.

Reporting guidelines by the WHO

What do we do if a suicide takes place? Below are some of the guidelines by the WHO for reporting and discussing suicide. As responsible individuals, we should follow them while talking with the media, writing on social media platforms or discussing it with our friends and colleagues.

i. Avoid saying 'committed'; instead say 'died'. by suicide.[55] The word 'commit' conveys the shame and an act of wrongdoing and is used to describe unlawful acts. It suggests that the person who passed away was a perpetrator and not a victim. When we say 'die by' instead, criminal intent attached is removed, leaving more room for understanding the illness and the circumstances which led to the suicide.
ii. Don't use sensationalist language.
iii. Include helpline numbers while writing articles.
iv. Don't give too many details.
v. Take particular care in reporting and discussing celebrity suicides.
vi. Educate the public about myths surrounding suicide.
vii. Exercise caution in using images.
viii. Avoid discussing the methods of suicide.
ix. Focus on life, not death.

Currently, we know a lot about suicide and its dynamics, but several of its aspects are still a mystery. By putting more attention, by spreading awareness and by conducting more studies in this area, I believe we will be able to reduce its frequency in the community. We must try to prevent every suicide wherever possible. Problems are temporary, and their solutions also need to be temporary. *Suicide is a permanent solution to a temporary problem.*

---

[55]Holmes, Lindsay, 'Why You Should Stop Saying 'Committed Suicide'", *Huffpost*, 26 March 2019, https://bit.ly/3qhs98P. Accessed on 21 March 2022.

8
I CAN SURVIVE THE PANDEMIC

The last two years have been perhaps the toughest in recent times for the global population. We could not have imagined even in our wildest dreams the circumstances we are living in today. There is probably not a single person whose life has not been affected, directly or indirectly, by the Covid-19 pandemic. For many families, the effect of this pandemic has been devastating, especially for those who lost a young family member or the breadwinner to the virus. As the pandemic evolved, so did the challenges. Different age groups were faced with different challenges. Here are the events that I saw unfolding.

2020: The pandemic strikes

When the first lockdown was announced in India in March 2020 and before we actually knew what direction this pandemic would take, many of us found the first three weeks quite relaxing and creative. On social media, everyone spread their wings when it came to trying new hobbies and cooking new dishes. But slowly, the picture began to change. The leisurely days spent at home turned into forced isolations, mental relaxation changed to constant worry and many stressors took a toll on our mental health.

Chief among these stressors were:

- **Staying away from loved ones**: Multiple lockdowns, travel bans and the terror of contracting the virus while travelling was so great that many people stayed away from their loved ones, which actually triggered much stress and anxiety, and even depression.
- **Social isolation**: We humans are social animals. Socializing is essential for our proper functioning. Simple things like dressing up for work and meeting our friends and colleagues over coffee can uplift our spirits. Home confinement because of the lockdown led to boredom, monotony and pent-up emotions. More cases of anger outbursts and intimate partner violence were reported as a result of that.[56]
- **Disruption of routine**: After the multiple lockdowns and work from home (WFH) continued indefinitely, most of us suffered from poor routines. We were waking up later than usual and having breakfast at odd hours. There was a tendency to work longer hours and often go to bed later than usual. The fixed-hour work schedule in pre-Covid-19 times, which was very helpful in maintaining a rhythm and balance, went for a toss.
- **Financial cuts and/or job losses for many**: The gravity of this problem was staggering. As per the Centre for Monitoring Indian Economy (CMIE), almost 12.2 crore Indians lost their jobs during Covid-19.[57] Many companies

---

[56] S. Nair, Vasundharaa and Debanjan Chatterjee, 'Crisis Within the Walls: Rise of Intimate Partner Violence During the Pandemic, Indian Perspectives', *Frontiers in Global Women's Health*, 28 May 2021, https://bit.ly/3qpOUY7. Accessed on 21 March 2022.

[57] 'Data | An estimated 12.2 crore Indians lost their jobs during the coronavirus lockdown in April: CMIE', *The Hindu*, 7 May 2020, https://bit.ly/3IpKYNd. Accessed on 21 March 2022.

refused increments to their employees; many others faced the constant stress of impending layoffs and downsizing decisions by employers.
- **Lack of recreation opportunities and monotony**: We were and are still turning to laptops, mobiles and television sets—essentially all electronic gadgets—for work, for recreation, for information and to help others as well. All other recreational opportunities such as visiting malls, taking a stroll in a park, travelling for pleasure, visiting friends and relatives, attending social gatherings and eating out were out of question when the cases were at their peak, and many people are in fact still avoiding these from fear of contracting Covid-19.
- **Virtual fatigue**: With the onset of the pandemic, most people in the private sector were asked to work from home. Millions of people all over the world are still continuing with the WFH model. Children have been attending virtual school/online classes since the beginning of the pandemic.

   What happens while working virtually is conversation, not communication. We listen to each other, but non-verbal cues such as expressions and body language may not be always clear, and to read those our brain has to make a lot more effort than usual.

   Excessive self-consciousness because of the camera and the background set-up of the house is common in virtual calls, and many people even face embarrassing issues due to home situations and may have to be extra alert during official meetings. Connectivity issues and dropped calls add to the stress of the experience. Eye strain, brain fatigue, and aching joints and muscles due to overstimulation and from sitting in one place for longer hours are also problems that many faced.

- **Change of plans and delays in achieving goals**: Many youngsters I know had to change their plans of studying abroad as exams got delayed or cancelled for an entire academic year. School authorities were worried about the thwarted academic growth of many students. Although virtual schooling is a boon in the pandemic, the effects of normal schooling are far better when it comes to the child's academic and overall development.
- **Disruption of personal goals**: Many marriage plans got postponed due to multiple lockdowns, while many others had to abruptly switch to a small-scale affair from a planned grand wedding.
- **Lack of space and boundaries**: Not only the working population, homemakers too faced this problem. All members staying under one roof 24/7, often resulted in a lack of space. With the children at school and husbands at work, many women got their much-needed time and space for some hours in the day. After the start of the pandemic, many of my female patients complained, 'My husband works from the bedroom, the children attend school from their bedroom and my in-laws are always in the hall. I have to attend to all their needs and work more than usual as the house help is not allowed entry to the society. Where is my space? Where is my time?' The working population is annoyed as well by the overwork they have to do and the constant intrusion by other family members. Many are working from the space not conducive to working for a longer time.
- **Infodemic**: Another growing element of the pandemic was the 'infodemic'. People were getting stressed and anxious due to baseless and fake information doing the rounds on social media. The information circulated was possibly incorrect and without a verified source or from the authorities in that

area. Such information created unnecessary panic among those who read or heard about it.
- **Uncertainty**: The issue hovering over our heads was the big cloud of uncertainty. We still don't know which direction this pandemic will take in the future and for how long the current circumstances will continue. It has surprised us with new waves whenever we thought the horror was almost over.

2021: More bad news

In 2021, when the vaccines were made widely available, there was a strong hope that the end of this pandemic was near. But what happened actually? Early in the first-half of the year came the second wave, aggressively claiming many lives, including youngsters. This brought a new set of challenges.

- **The fear of losing loved ones**: As Covid-19 took a malignant turn, not sparing even the young, the majority of us were all the more worried for ourselves and for our loved ones.
- **Coming out of grief**: The deaths caused by Covid-19 are called 'bad deaths' in medicine, as they happen in the isolation ward of a hospital set-up, may happen unpredictably and without any major morbid illness, without relatives around. No communal mourning is possible even later, which makes coming out of grief all the more difficult.
- **The fear of contracting Covid-19**: This happened when unforeseen after-effects and complications of Covid-19 and its treatment were being seen. These included mucormycosis (also known as black fungus), blood clots, strokes and heart attacks.
- **Unavailability of treatment**: This problem was greatly aggravated in the second wave, which saw a breakdown of

available medical resources and treatment in various parts of the country. I personally know many patients whose relatives breathed their last at home or on the way to the hospital. I also know some patients who died in the hospital when they did not get the required supply of oxygen due to a dearth of oxygen cylinders or did not get the required medicines on time.

- **Post-Covid-19 complications**: 10–20 per cent of the people who were affected with Covid-19 have long Covid-19, meaning the complications lasted for a few months. Symptoms of long Covid-19 could be issues with the voice and problem in swallowing, breathing issues, joint pain, headache, fatigue, loss of taste, and issues with memory and concentration. As per studies, 30–40 per cent of them developed depression and anxiety during/after the infection period.[58] The fear of impending complications and the trauma of social isolation were common too. Some even faced stigmatization from the community. All of these led to depression and anxiety and still continues to affect patients.

2022: Hope at last?

After the second wave, the case count started falling, the vaccination drive sped up and many of us felt that Covid-19 was almost gone. But the cases started rising again in early 2022 and the third wave hit us, although many patients got a milder version of the disease due to the Omicron variant. But many still needed hospitalization. Many succumbed to gloom

---

[58] Mazza, Mario Gennaro et al., 'Anxiety and depression in COVID-19 survivors: Role of inflammatory and clinical predictors', *Brain, Behavior, and Immunity*, 30 July 2020, https://bit.ly/3qm2AUd. Accessed on 21 March 2022.

after the partial lockdown was announced again.

This cycle of moving cities for work, attempting to regularize our life and then being locked in again with the onset of the new wave is mentally exhausting. These last two years were emotionally taxing for each of us, irrespective of age and occupation, and really tested our resilience.

Responding to the pandemic

Let's look at the graph describing the common responses to the pandemic:

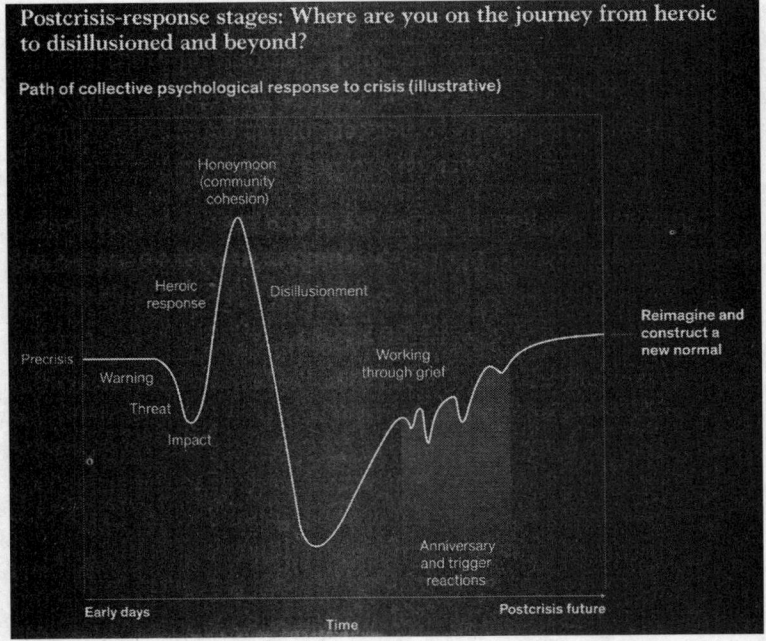

Source: Smet, Aaron De et al., 'Overcoming pandemic fatigue: How to reenergize organizations for the long run', McKinsey & Company, 25 November 2020.

Whenever we faced a threat before the pandemic, we responded with an alarm reaction or adrenaline reaction (heroic response) by preparing ourselves for a crisis. When the first wave was in full swing, we supported each other using various means. When cases dropped, we started meeting again in small gatherings, and there was a phase of relief ('honeymoon'). With the second wave, when major resources were breaking down, there was a phase of disillusionment, where the damage dashed the hopes and positivity. The recovery from the trauma began, along with gradually managing the grief from the loss of loved ones. This also involved trying to come back to a sense of normalcy in the new circumstances, with some losses and accepting the uncertainty. In the whole process, as much as 75 per cent of the American population reported burnouts in the private sector, while in Asia-Pacific, it was as much as 50 per cent.[59]

Effects on mental health

Corona-phobia was a new psychiatric illness falling within the anxiety–OCD spectrum, which was newly diagnosed in clinical practice during the pandemic. It is characterized by the following symptoms:

- Uncontrollable anxiety
- Fears are out of proportion to the actual danger
- The fear and anxiety are intense and persistent (lasting weeks to months)

---

[59] 'Workplace Burnout Survey: Burnout without borders', Deloitte, https://bit.ly/3qodjgF. Accessed on 21 March 2022; de Smet, Aaron et al., 'How to reenergize your organization to overcome pandemic fatigue', McKinsey & Company, 1 March 2021, https://mck.co/3wka11X. Accessed on 21 March 2022.

- It's hard to stop worrying about coronavirus
- They actively avoid situations (for instance, places, people and activities), even those that are possibly safe
- They spend a lot of time monitoring their body for signs and symptoms or searching the Internet about the virus
- They become overly obsessive about cleaning, washing and decontaminating

I know many people who were mopping the floor of their home with sanitizers for months and months, obsessively cleaning all door knobs every hour and rubbing sanitizers on their hands every few minutes without going out of the house. These people sat at home for months and got more anxious and depressed with time.

Corona-phobia needs to be treated like any anxiety disorder, and patients got better with medications, counselling and reassurance.

The pandemic triggered a '35% rise in anxiety and depression each in Indians', states *Lancet*.[60]

Due to all the challenges and the constant fear, the instances of depression and anxiety disorders are increasing greatly, in both people who have been affected by Covid-19 and those who haven't. Our brain is good at responding to short bursts of stress, but it's not as good at operating under constant, low-grade pressure. A lot of our brain's capacity is used up subconsciously in handling this constant threat and dealing with the routine challenges, hence we obviously need to make a greater effort to focus in this pandemic period. Lack of productivity, low focus, poor communication and poor

---

[60]'Covid-19 pandemic triggered 35% rise in anxiety, depression in Indians, says Lancet report', *The Times of India*, 9 October 2021, https://bit.ly/3JmthPX. Accessed on 21 March 2022.

- According to various studies, sleep disturbances are now found in 40–45 per cent of the general population, while it was 25–30 per cent in pre-Covid-19 times.[61] They are equally prevalent among all age groups, including children. Sleep disturbances may happen due to excessive worry, disturbed routine, lack of physical exercise and excessive use of gadgets.
- Behavioural problems such as anger dysregulation issues and increased violence are on the rise due to a disturbed routine, job loss, overwork at home, increased vigilance on other family members and isolation. Pent-up negative emotions can lead to outbursts.
- Addictions such as alcohol could be the easy answer to sleeplessness, boredom and lack of recreation opportunities, so addiction cases increased substantially during this period. The use of other substances also increased to break the boredom and to gain some stimulation for work.
- Extreme reactions such as hysteria and attack of psychosis have happened to some people after a diagnosis of Covid-19.
- People have suffered from heart issues or sudden blood

---

[61]Jahrami, Haitham et al., 'Sleep problems during the COVID-19 pandemic by population: a systematic review and meta-analysis', *Journal of Clinical Sleep Medicine*, February 2021, 17(2): 299–313, https://bit.ly/3ug0whC. Accessed on 21 March 2022; Bruni, Oliviero et al., 'Changes in sleep patterns and disturbances in children and adolescents in Italy during the Covid-19 outbreak', *Sleep Medicine*, 9 February 2021, https://bit.ly/3IqBph5. Accessed on 21 March 2022.

pressure changes as well, which added to the morbidity and mortality due to Covid-19.

And these were not directly caused by Covid-19! Fear and anxiety make things especially difficult for patients who have tested positive for Covid-19. It's essential to curb our fears to lead a near-normal life.

Issues specific to certain populations

Frontline workers: When the waves were in full swing, most of us worked much beyond our capacity and in an atmosphere of constant fear and threat. Many frontline workers succumbed to Covid-19, which they contracted at work. While many of the other professions had the option of working from home, doctors and frontline workers had no choice. Working in full personal protective equipment (PPE) kit for most of the time at the hospital was not easy, wearing N95 masks for eight to 10 hours was suffocating, and many of us had to delay bathroom breaks due to our PPE kits. Much time was wasted and is still being spent in hygiene rituals we need to follow after returning from work.

Most of us were concerned that our family members would contract Covid-19 because of us. Many of us suffered from social ostracism when it came to get-togethers because of the fear that we might be carriers of the infection. Many of us suffered from sleeplessness, burnouts, anxiety and depression during this period when the caseload was very high. In the second wave, when there was a resource crunch, most of us (doctors) were seeing Covid-19 patients every day, irrespective of our specializations. Witnessing the massive loss of human life in a short span of time caused much trauma. Almost all of us got several calls a day asking for help with arranging oxygen cylinders, remdesivir or hospital beds. Many of us suffered from compassion fatigue, meaning feelings of numbness or a vacuum even after seeing the critical patients. Empathy fatigue or compassion fatigue was a sign of secondary trauma and possible depression.

Women: In general, women faced a much higher workload and suffered from a lack of personal space and boundaries. Many were victims of domestic violence, while others had less secure jobs and suffered from more job losses. Biologically, too, women experience greater fears and anxieties, and these worsened during this period. They were tasked with co-attending online classes with their children and with engaging the bored and irritated children at home. Many suffered from self-neglect and many reported having experienced cyber abuse.

Children: This group suffered the most during the pandemic, but this suffering is under-recognized. They often don't have direct access to information, they need reassurance multiple times for various reasons, are sometimes easy punchbags for many issues (which may trigger a guilt cycle later in parents) and they need constant change as they get bored easily.

Many of them are suffering owing to sleep disturbances, anxiety and depression issues. In the teenage population, gadget addiction issues, addiction to other illicit substances and behavioural problems such as anger outbursts are also significant problems.

Geriatric population: Being homebound for most of the time, as Covid-19 is more deadly for old people, this population faced a disturbed routine. They were much more bored at home, as many have poor sensory faculties such as weak vision and hearing and aren't able to enjoy virtual entertainment and reading. Existing illnesses worsened in many due to a sedentary lifestyle, and there was a steady rise in stress levels, leading to a worsening of diabetes and blood pressure issues. Many were scared to visit the hospital for fear of contracting Covid-19 and suffered for longer periods. More issues related to forgetfulness and confusion were reported due to less stimulation to mind and staying at home for long periods of time.

Although we sigh with relief when the wave recedes, with every new wave the vicious cycle of stress sets in. Experts around the world are still not sure about the possible mutant strains and what the duration of this pandemic could be. Its effects could even last a decade because of the damage it has done and also the impending uncertainty. Many things are beyond our control when it comes to the pandemic, but there are a few things that can be controlled in addition to standard social distancing, wearing masks and washing hands frequently. We can keep our fears under control, accept the current uncertainty and lead a better-quality life with greater productivity by developing better coping mechanisms.

Maintaining mental balance

Change your 'information diet'

- **Understanding the difference between 'news' and 'views'：** I remember as kids, we usually watched only Doordarshan, very few had a cable connection with other channels. On Doordarshan, a presenter would read a bulletin with important news with a near-blank expression. This used to be a matter of 20 minutes, every morning and every evening. This news was always thoroughly verified, but the impact it had was very limited. Now with news channels

running 24 hours, news is still a two-liner, but the views of different people make it expand. As viewers, we need to pick out the news in all that matter and understand that the rest are views, which appeal to emotions. In fact, restricting the exposure to only headlines once in a day when feeling stressed out is quite helpful.
- **Getting facts from the authorities concerned**: There is much information going around about the virus and its treatment, and also about the vaccines. Verifying this information with the authorities concerned to get to the actual facts can greatly reduce fear and anxiety.
- **Problem versus solutions**: Often thinking about how big the problem is doesn't serve any purpose beyond a point, and we just get more disturbed if we focus on it. Instead, once we know the magnitude of the problem, we can start searching for possible solutions that are in our control.

Factors under our control and beyond our control

- Think about this and distinguish clearly between the two kinds of factors. This can really make a difference to our mental state.
- If the problem or part of the problem is under your control, please do something about it.
- If it's beyond your control, remove it from your mind as well.
- To get rid of unwanted thoughts and worries, practise thought-stopping methods, such as the rubber band method, which are discussed earlier in the book.

Burden versus decision

When we say 'I don't want to, but I have to', this negative thinking tends to put hurdles in our path. Some things are inevitable or you need to follow without question. In such cases, tell your mind that you choose to do them, as this reduces your resistance and smoothens the process. So, replace the thought with, 'I am doing this because it's good for my life'. For example, you might say, 'I choose to stay home because it helps me stay safe.'

The moment you choose to do something instead of being forced into it, it doesn't feel like a burden.

How to handle children

- **Understand and acknowledge their frustration**: Kids are affected even more than us by the circumstances. They are in need of constant change and are more prone to boredom. Because of the pandemic, they can't meet their friends or play outdoors. Their routine has been disturbed. It's difficult for them to stay at home for extended periods. So, understanding their frustration and acknowledging it shows that you understand what they are going through. This is the first step to better bonding during this period.
- **Bridge the gap by sharing from both sides**: Ask them what they want to know about the pandemic, tell what you know about the pandemic, discuss other questions and listen to them if they want to share something. Hear out what information they have and correct them if needed and educate them as per their age.
- **Address their fears and worries**: Address even simple questions like 'Does it mean this year my birthday won't be celebrated?' or 'Has something happened to us?'. Give honest answers and assure them that the situation can be overcome together.
- **Strategic engagements**: Engage them in games and puzzles, which involve problem-solving. Give them the responsibility of small everyday chores and teach them some art form.

Ways to combat virtual fatigue

Even if we are able to rein in the pandemic, virtual fatigue is going to be an issue in the future, as many companies have decided to allow their employees to work from home indefinitely. Finding ways to manage virtual fatigue is very much needed. Here are few helpful tips:

- Take virtual time off. Take a break of 5 minutes every hour while working.
- Turn off notifications, if possible, when you get up from work.
- Block calendar slots in advance for necessary leaves or breaks.
- Set a deadline and create an agenda for every video call, so that overshooting due to initial casual chatter can be avoided.
- Turn off your camera when not needed.
- Use regular phone calls or emails whenever possible.
- Do eye exercises. Follow the rule of 20-20-20: look at a 20-feet distance for 20 seconds every 20 minutes.
- Stay hydrated. Drink a minimum of 2–2.5 litres of water every day. Along with many benefits, this also helps keep brain fatigue at bay.
- Clear your digital and physical clutter from your workspace, as it gives clarity and reduces jitteriness.
- Revamp your room by making small changes. Keep indoor plants or fresh flowers on your desk. Ensure you have adequate ventilation and lighting, as this can reduce feelings of gloom.

Maintaining positivity when you have Covid-19

- Switch off news from all sources till you recover.
- Stop checking your vitals and saturation beyond the frequency recommended by your doctor.
- Maintain a positive self-dialogue. For example, 'I am recovering, I am getting better', and so on.
- Play the flute, sing and inflate balloons—these are good exercises for the lungs and helps relieve anxiety.
- Challenge your fears. When you think, 'What if it takes a serious turn?', look at the statistics of Covid-19, look at your vital statistics too. Challenge your emotional reactions with rational thoughts.
- Watch positive movies.
- Reflect on life. As the saying goes, when you cannot go out, go inside. Think about the call of your inner being.
- Create memorabilia. Go through old photos and add your personal note to each.
- Journaling can help. Writing down your thoughts and activities often leads you to understand your triggers. You can discuss these with your family members, doctors or counsellors.
- When you have recovered sufficiently and regained enough energy, talk to people with a positive mindset.
- Get adequate sleep. Cell-mediated immunity functions well when we sleep. Sleep also helps in repairing wear and tear. Sleep on your sides or in prone position.
- Positivity has a great effect on Covid-19 recovery. The love hormone, oxytocin, plays a big role in preventing a cytokine storm, which is a major complication that doctors fear. Immunity improves with lower stress levels, and leads to a higher NK cell count. NK cells are our fighter cells,

which help protect us from diseases. Lower inflammation leads to fewer cytokines. The inflammation in the body is the cause of many complications, and it definitely reduces if one is happy and positive. Positivity also leads to better control over blood pressure. Happiness and positivity curb adrenaline and other stress hormones, which keep the mind and body calmer and promote recovery.

Coping mechanisms in these times of uncertainty

- Have a positive person as a vent buddy. Psychiatry says that as we age, we stop making new friends. But all of us have a bunch of good friends. Have a vent buddy who has a more positive state of mind than you and who can help relieve your stress. Talk to each other at least once a week. This should be other than family members.
- Read and circulate stories about corona warriors. The media banks on what appeals most to our emotions, and that is fear. But there are people who have won very difficult battles, and we need to spread their stories. Such news spreads positivity.
- Do mindfulness exercises such as the 5-4-3-2-1 coping technique. Whenever you feel anxious, look for five things you can see, four things you can touch, three things you can hear, two things you can smell and one thing you can taste. Such activities bring the mind to the present.
- Don't indulge in alcohol or over-the-counter drugs. Although they may look like an easy answer to anxiety, they take a serious toll on our health in the long run. And once the addiction sets in, getting rid of it is altogether a different battle.
- Find better ways of venting. Scribbling or running up and down the stairs a few times can help release negative energy.
- Use affirmations and autosuggestions. The conscious mind

is a thinker, while the unconscious is a prover. If you say something again and again to yourself, your body and mind will listen to it and follow it. Say 'I am good, I am healthy, I am happy' many times a day, and you will see the results soon.
- Challenge your fear and keep a contingency plan ready. Being positive and hopeful doesn't mean we should not keep our contingency plan ready. I remember watching a web series recently. A character asks his friend, 'If you are so sure you want to be an IAS officer, then why are you appearing for other exams?' The friend replies, 'Plan B is there for balance!' If the fear sounds logical, keep a contingency plan ready. If you have a plan B ready, your anxiety definitely reduces greatly. For example, make a list of your contacts by writing down the numbers of important people in your life, friends who will be there to help you anytime and numbers of ambulances and hospitals for when the need arises.
- Help others but remember your limitations and respect them. There are times when you can help and times when you cannot. Don't feel guilty if sometimes you have to say no. Respect your limitations to avoid feeling tired and stressed.

Remember that times of crisis are not times for perfection

- Division of labour is very much needed in the house, as the workload has increased multifold during the pandemic. To keep mental and physical fatigue under control, division of labour is necessary. It's better to involve all members of the family in taking up small or big responsibilities and daily chores.
- Learn to say no. Major issues arise when we don't know how to say no, whether at the professional or personal front.

If something is affecting your mental peace, please say no.
- Keep some me time. Spend 15–20 minutes just with yourself every day. Sit in the balcony, smell your coffee, go for walks alone. This helps in keeping our connection with ourselves intact and in restoring the connect if it's lost. It's very important for preventing depression in the long run.
- Stop being harsh on yourself. Surviving the pandemic is enough. Gaining a few kilos or scoring less in an exam should not make you self-critical. We all are going through stress, and such drawbacks should be taken in your stride.
- Make sure you remain a good parent. Times of crisis are not times for perfection, and this applies to parenting too. Don't give importance to your child scoring a few marks less or a couple of anger outbursts from them due to boredom. Be there for them for their basic needs as well as emotional needs.
- Take the time for self-care and appreciation. Pat yourself on the back every day for facing challenges and for not losing your cool. Appreciate small wins for you and your family.
- Connect with people of the same age and gender. As age advances, we find a better connect with people of the same age and gender as we have lots of common things to share and discuss. Connect in person when possible or have virtual meetings.
- Exercise and take in fresh air regularly. It's essential to exercise to release anti-stress hormones and keep immunity intact. You should do it in fresh air if possible. Even the verandah of your house is fine. Fresh air acts like magic on a tensed mind. A minimum of 15–20 minutes of exposure to it is needed, no matter what the weather.
- Give everyone the benefit of the doubt, whether at home or at the workplace. Everyone is going through some or the

other stress due to the pandemic, so less judging and more acceptance is needed.
- Take one day at a time and follow a routine. Thinking about the distant future only increases feelings of uncertainty and brings more anxiety. Instead, living one day at a time and following a semi-fixed routine is better for the current situation.

We still don't have answers to certain questions, such as when this pandemic will end, when our will life go back to what it was in pre-Covid-19 times and if we will enjoy freedom in its truest sense. But one thing is for sure, that every storm blows over and this is the law of the universe, of utpatti-sthiti-laya—whatever has begun has to face an end. The same logic applies to this pandemic too. Until then, let's focus on one tool we have—our positive attitude. As psychiatrist Dr Viktor Frankl has written in his famous book *Man's Search for Meaning*, 'Everything can be taken from a man but one thing: the last of the human freedom—to choose one's attitude in any given set of circumstances, to choose one's own way.'[62]

---

[62] Frankl, Viktor E., *Man's Search for Meaning: The classic tribute to hope from the Holocaust*, RHUK; Exported edition (2008).

ACKNOWLEDGEMENTS

As I look back on the journey of writing this book, I remember how the doubts I had. Will I be able to commit the time? Will I be able to put in the efforts required to conceptualize and write this book? Will this affect my hospital and home responsibilities? But the actual journey was very interesting and smooth, thanks to the help received from several people.

Thank you, Yamini, for constantly encouraging me and giving me flexibility in conceptualizing the book. I could not have asked for a better editor than Aurodeep—thank you for your inputs and edits. The experience of working with Rupa Publications was amazing, thank you.

A special thanks to my husband Dr Amit Gaikwad, for his suggestions, for motivating me to write in moments of self-doubt, helping me with the technical domains and taking on extra responsibilities at home. This book would not have been completed in time without my four-year-old's understanding and patience; Aarush, love you for not complaining when Mummy was busy. My parents Adv. Anjali Joshi and the late Adv. Arvind Joshi, thank you for teaching me to think beyond myself and express myself freely.

Many of my colleagues, friends and teachers have contributed to this book, directly and indirectly. I am grateful to all of you.

Thank you to the readers of my previous two books which were published in Marathi. Your comments and feedback motivated me to write further.

How can I forget my patients! It was only because of you that I could see questions and problems beyond the superficial world, which helped me in understanding psychiatry better. Thank you for opening your heart to me and helping me broaden my horizons.

Almighty God, thank you for everything.